Always Being Reformed
A Celebration of the 500th Anniversary of the Protestant Reformation

House to House
PRESS

Always Being Reformed

Copyright © 2018 by House to House Press, a division of H&E Publishing.

All rights reserved. This book or any portion thereof may not be reproduced or used in any manner whatsoever without the express written permission of the author(s) except for the use of brief quotations.

ISBN 978-1-989174-08-1
First Print 2018
Printed in Canada

Dedication
To Christ's Church in Peterborough,
whom He loved and gave Himself up for.

Contents

Preface.. vii
Chance Faulkner

1 A History of the Reformation............................ 1
Jason Belgrave

2 Scripture Alone... 19
Derek Green

3 Christ Alone... 41
Josh Anderson

4 Faith Alone.. 53
Josh Anderson

5 Grace Alone... 65
Alexander Kloosterman

6 Glory Alone... 91
Rylan R.P. Auger

7 Semper Reformanda................................... 109
Alexander Kloosterman

8 William Tyndale....................................... 121
Derek Green

Preface

This book is the fruit of a series of messages presented at the 2017 Peterborough Reformation Conference—an event which celebrated the 500th anniversary of the Protestant Reformation. The conference saw three local congregations (Braidwood Bible Chapel, The Gathering, and Westmount Bible Chapel) come together to be reminded of the central tenets of the historical movement which recovered the heart of the Bible's teaching for the church. During this time, our local congregations had the opportunity to learn from gifted teachers, as well as enjoying fellowship with believers outside of their own local churches.

Those messages, which make up the substance of this book, have been gathered together as a kind of ebenezer for our local churches; both to remember our time together and cherish the work of God as it culminated in the person and work of our Lord Jesus Christ. Though the content of these chapters are in no way exhaustive of the subject, we hope they will serve to edify and build up the saints, as they are found true to the Bible's teaching.

Jason Belgrave begins the first chapter with "A History of the Reformation." Here he provides a survey of Church history spanning from the early church to the 16th century, during which he attempts to answer several questions: What were the main issues which led up to the Reformation? When did it begin? And what legacy of writings do we possess from this period?

In chapter 2, Derek Green works through the first Sola, "Scripture Alone." Here he considers the doctrine of Sola Scriptura under the headings of inspiration, inerrancy, clarity, and sufficiency, and demonstrates how the doctrine of Sola Scriptura worked itself out in the preaching ministries of the Reformers. He then considers why this is so important in our day.

Josh Anderson teaches on "Christ Alone" in chapter 3, and focuses his attention on two essential realities: 1) The exclusivity of Christ's identity as the unique Son of God, and 2) The sufficiency of Christ's work as the unique Son of God. Because of the exclusive identity and sufficient work of Jesus Christ, the believer can be absolutely confident that God loves them and is for them.

Chapter 4 focuses on "Faith Alone." Here, Josh shows us that faith in Christ is the only way for one to be justified before God, and also explores the relationship between faith and works.

Chapter 5 is by Alexander Kloosterman on, "Grace Alone." He shows that our fallen and lost condition makes us people who love self-exaltation and boasting—qualities which blind us to God's grace. He takes us through Ephesians 2:1-10 and seeks to demonstrate: 1. That sinners are in need of salvation. 2. That the cause of our salvation is through grace alone. 3. The nature of the gracious work of God in salvation. 4. The end goal of our salvation.

In chapter 6, Rylan Auger teaches on the subject of "God's Glory Alone." In this chapter, he provides us with a definition of glory, namely, "that the glory of God is seen in who God is and what God does." He also addresses several questions such as: Why is God glorified through our salvation? What compels us to praise God for his Glory?

In the end, Rylan concludes that God's glory is worthy of praise "because our joy in God's glory, in God himself, naturally overflows in His praise."

In chapter 7, Alexander gives an exhortation on what it means to always be reforming. Here, he shows that true believers always put themselves under the scrutiny of the Scriptures because life is one of faith and repentance. The fruit of a life of faith and repentance is deep humility and a profound unity with other believers.

Chapter 8 concludes with a biography of William Tyndale. Here, Derek Green provides a brief sketch of a man who gave his life to making God's Word accessible to God's people.

I hope these messages encourage and strengthen you in Christ—our only hope in life and death.

Chance Faulkner
Peterborough, Ontario
August 3, 2018

1

A History of the Reformation

Jason Belgrave

For many, the classic scene of Martin Luther nailing his 95 Theses to the Wittenberg Cathedral door *is* the history of the Reformation. It's true that in many ways this event became the epicentre of the Reformation. However, this event did not exist in a vacuum. We tend to think of the Reformation as a time where history was progressing one way, then suddenly a few men, lead by Martin Luther, got together and said, "We need to do things differently." But Luther was not nailing a new way of doing things to the door. The Reformation has its name for a reason; it was not the *formation* of something new but a *re-formation* of something that already existed.

History reveals that the Reformation was, and is, much more than that moment at the Wittenberg door. As we explore the history of the Reformation, we'll answer three questions: 1) When did the Reformation begin? 2) What sparked the Reformation? And 3) What was the main issue of the Reformation? These answers will help us to separate perception from reality and bring us to a better understanding of the heart of the Reformation.

As we study world history, it's important to remember that God's word itself contains much history. To that end, the inerrant word of God and what it tells us of His work in the world must inform our understanding of our own history.

What's more, all of history has a context. Consider the World Wars. Countries do not one day just wake up and decide to fight one another; there were days and weeks and years leading up to the battles that ensued. In the same way, events going farther back than you'd think lead up to that day we now call "Reformation Day," October 31, 1517. In fact, we can go all the way back to the beginning of the church to see how we arrived at that moment in time. In the book of Acts, we can see the principles behind what we call the "five solas": Christ alone, Scripture alone, Faith alone, Grace alone, to the Glory of God alone.

The True Church (30 AD)
"When the day of Pentecost arrived, they were all together in one place...." (Acts 2:1). This day of Pentecost was the true birth of the church, as the Holy Spirit came down to the apostles. We see what the church was like in those early stages: "They devoted themselves to the apostles' teaching and the fellowship, to the breaking of the bread and the prayers" (Acts 2:42). The true church, coming off a powerful start through the power of the Holy Spirit, was characterized by a devotion to the Word, the teaching of the apostles. What was this teaching? We see an example of Peter and John's teaching a few chapters later:

> This Jesus is the stone that was rejected by you the builders which has become the cornerstone and there is salvation in no one else. For there is no other name

under heaven given among men by which we must be saved (Acts 4:11).

And so we see our first sola just a mere two chapters after the birth of the Church: no one else saves but *Christ alone*.

Turning to Acts 7, we see Stephen, one of the first deacons, a servant of the early church, standing before an angry mob and giving them a history lesson. He walked them through Scripture, from Abraham to the Righteous One (Acts 7:1-53), showing them that as much as they may try to fight it, God's truth is found in *Scripture alone*.

Stephen wasn't trying to be clever or relevant. Instead, before an angry mob, he stood reasoning on Scripture alone.

This was not the heart of men like Simon the Magician (Acts 8). He saw the work of the apostles and wanted the same power they had. The apostles instead gave him this rebuke: "You have neither part nor lot in this matter, for your heart is not right before God" (Acts 8:21). Here at the beginning of the church, people want to take the glory away from God and give it to man. However, note the rebuke from the apostles: *To the glory of God alone*.

Next we turn to Acts 15. The church has been birthed, it has faced persecution, and it has grown, but now they face an internal problem:

> But some men came down from Judea and were teaching the brothers, "unless you are circumcised according to the custom of Moses you cannot be saved" (Acts 15:1).

Suddenly, a new teaching is coming from inside the church: you must be circumcised in order to be saved. This directly contradicts what true Jewish people have always known, and what the Bible has always taught: "The righteous shall live by faith" (Habakkuk 2:4). Clearly, the early church was already in need of reform. The righteous live by faith, not by their works, including circumcision. The response of the church was swift: "The apostles and the elders were gathered to consider the matter" (Acts 15:6). They came together as a church and said, "Is this teaching so? Let's examine." And then, the action:

> And after there had been much debate, Peter stood up and said to them, "Brothers, you know that in the early days God made a choice among you, that by my mouth the Gentiles should hear the word of the gospel and believe. And God, who knows the heart, bore witness to them, by giving them the Holy Spirit just as he did to us, and he made no distinction between us and them, having cleansed their hearts by faith (Acts 15:7-9).

Do you see that? "No distinction between us and them," between Jew and Gentile, "having cleansed their hearts by faith." *Faith alone.* Yet another sola that has been present since the beginning of the church. "But we believe that we will be saved through the grace of the Lord Jesus, just as they will" (Acts 15:11). We will be saved through the grace of Christ, an amazing truth which we know as *grace alone.*

Scripture alone. Christ alone. Grace alone. Faith alone. To the Glory of God alone. That's the apostles' teaching. This was not a 16th century invention; it has been present since the very beginning of the church. Christianity has always been about these five solas. But we also see through this study of Acts that from the very beginning, this teaching has been under attack, and therefore we should not be surprised that it continues to be attacked to this very day.

The Persecuted Church (30–313 AD)

The early church was defined in many ways by persecution, and we see that throughout the book of Acts as well as in church history. Peter and John are arrested (Acts 4); the apostles are arrested again (Acts 5); Stephen is stoned at the hands of the Jews (Acts 7); James the apostle is killed and Peter is imprisoned (Acts 12); Paul and Silas are beaten and put into prison in Philippi (Acts 16). This kind of persecution continued throughout the New Testament era and beyond. The emperor Nero was a famous 1st century emperor famed for his persecution of Christians in 64 AD. Nero was relentless in his attack on Christians. History tells us that he very likely was looking for a scapegoat for his own power and his own "real estate" business in Rome, and he found none better than Christians to use at his will, usually by the stake. Then there was the emperor Domitian at the end of the 1st century. He was the one who exiled the apostle John to the island of Patmos, where he wrote the book of Revelation. As we move into the beginning of the second century, the magistrate Pliny writes to the emperor Trajan and basically says, *I don't know if you know what's going on in this corner of the empire, but Christians are being killed by the thousands daily.* Daily. Later in that century, 161 AD, was Marcus Aurelius, who famously bound one of the church fathers, Polycarp. He demanded that Polycarp, a downstream disciple of the apostle John, abandon Christ. Think about it. All he needed to do was renounce the foundation of Christ alone, and stand on some other foundation. Polycarp's response was this:

> 86 years I have served Him and He never once wronged me. How can I blaspheme my King now who saved me?[1]

Polycarp, like the saints before him, clung to "Christ alone" even to the point of death! Can you imagine feeling the flame lick your feet? But he would not recant. *Christ alone.* This is nothing new— it's the one true teaching that has always been. And yet Polycarp, like countless others, would lose their lives for this truth.

You would think that at this point in history, given all the persecution that the early church faced, that the church would die out. That's of course what many emperors wanted, but that's not what happened. In fact, in the middle of the third century, 249 AD, it was recorded that pagan temples in Rome were the ones being drained. The temples were empty, and the people were going to church instead! The churches were actually overflowing in the third century. Renald Showers, the great Jewish historian of our age, gives us this quote:

> When we think about that time from approximately 250 to 311 AD, government persecution is planned and vigorous. Officials throughout the empire are ordered to arrest Christians and give them this ultimatum, "Deny your faith in Jesus Christ or die."[2]

---

[1] John Foxe, *Foxe's Book of Martyrs* (Uhrichsville, OH: Barour Publishing Inc., 2001), 18.

[2] Showers, Renald. 1999–2000. Persecution. *Israel My Glory*, Insert B.

It became official policy to destroy Christianity. Vast numbers of Christians refused to deny Jesus (we could say, refused to deny *Christ alone*) and therefore many became martyrs, often as public entertainment in large arenas. Yet the church grew stronger and expanded throughout the empire.

Amazing! And doesn't this challenge us as we sit here in 2017? We're in a time where many believe that church growth is all about being "relevant," yet there is nothing relevant about losing your life for Jesus. But that truth drew people to the church, to Christ. That is how He builds His church. The blood of the martyrs is what waters the church. No false teaching, no tradition, no emperor could extinguish the true church. Now at this point, let us remind ourselves of a few historical truths we've seen:

The teaching of the true church has always contained these five solas that we're looking at this weekend. That has always been part of the church. You don't need to dig up a great reformed book and brush up on your Latin or anything; you can open up your Bible anytime and find the five solas.

That teaching, those five solas, have always been under attack. We see that in Scripture, and we see that in church history. But we can also see this: that persecution did not choke out the truth. The attacks, in fact, did not only grow the church, but stood to sharpen and strengthen the church as well. This will become clear as we move on.

The State-Church (313–590 AD)

A young emperor named Constantine is marching his army toward Rome. Why? Because there was a renegade Caesar-type individual there, Maxentius, who had set up a post in Rome. He's ruthless, he's tyrannical, and Constantine, like a good leader, wanted to make things right. The rumor was that

Maxentius was using magic and dark arts, and Constantine was feeling very anxious on his way to face him. Until one day at sunset on the way to Rome, he looked up and in the sky he saw a cross. And he saw, reportedly, these words: "In this overcome." Supposedly, Jesus Himself was telling Constantine to go into battle, and he did just that. He met Maxentius at the outskirts of Rome, and he won. He liberated the people who were under tyranny of Maxentius. That huge military victory did more than just liberate them; it changed the landscape of the whole empire. And things changed for Constantine, not just politically, but personally.

After that military victory, Constantine began to alter the political landscape. He established a kingdom that was very favourable to the Christian worship of God, and *persecution gave way to privilege*. The Church was no longer hidden; now it was everywhere. For the next sixty-seven years, Christianity was brought into every facet of human life in the empire. Can you imagine it? From *persecution to the pedestal*. In 380 AD, Theodosius the Great actually made Christianity the official religion of the kingdom. Not only was it everywhere, it was legislated everywhere. To be a citizen of the state meant you were also a citizen of the church. The marriage of state and church had begun; the state church was born.

Now you might be thinking, "we could use some of that in 2017 in North America." You might be thinking that it sounds too good to be true, especially as you consider news items and political leaders today. Indeed, it sounds wonderful; it sounds just like the antidote for our society. But there is a problem. It may seem good from the standpoint of us in the church body, but it was never good for the one who was the head of the church. Jesus never said that this is the way the church should function. Remember Jesus' words when they brought Him a coin to try to trick Him. "Render to Caesar the things that are Caesar's, and to God the things that are God's" (Mark 12:17). As well, consider Jesus' plain teaching in the Upper Room: "You are not of the world" (John 15:19). We can cite 1 John 2, and we can go on and on. Jesus, the head of the church, is clear. As wonderful as the marriage of state and church may seem to us, we must remember when we go to the inerrant word of God, that's not what we find. Jesus is saying something very, very different. And things that are in not in the will of God usually don't fare well. Considering that, it's no surprise what happens next.

Over the years, the church-state marriage is firmly entrenched. *Spiritual leaders are also state leaders, priests are also politicians.* The church has divided interests, distractions. The responsibilities of the church and the state are all blended together. Corruption, it is no surprise, now enters the church, finds a hold and grows. During this time we find many of the unbiblical heresies springing up. To name a few: Baptismal regeneration. It's like citizenship papers, right? Baptism becomes your ticket "in." The veneration of Mary and the saints and relics becomes popular. Why? The Roman empire, and many empires, were all about worship. Just give me something to worship. We love to worship anything but the One that created us: virgin Mary, relics, saints, on and on it goes. All of these heresies are now coming into the church because of the marriage of church and state.

The ground is becoming fertile for false teaching. And yet there were attempts to right the ship, to try to get us back on course, and we are thankful for those. Famous councils were held during this time--the Council of Nicea (325 AD) and the Council of Ephesus (431 AD). Denying the deity of

Christ was the most significant heresy that was propagated at this time, that needed to be denied by these councils. While some key doctrines were defended, ultimately not all of them were able to hold on against the pressures that the church was facing from the state.

The key doctrines of the faith, the "good deposit" (2 Tim. 1:14), were slipping away because the interests of the world had crept into the church. The church that was flourishing for those first few centuries is now floundering. And that takes us to the next era.

The Medieval Church (590–1517 AD)

This is the period commonly known as "the Dark Ages." And it has that name for a reason—these times were very, very dark for the church. This is the period where Rome cements itself as the so-called head of the church, and what will become to be known as the Roman Catholic church. In the 11th century, the Eastern church split from the Roman church. But the Roman church dominates in the western world. This is also the period where we have the rise of Islam in the 7th century. That's important because it feeds right into the heart of the dark ages.

Many of the Middle Eastern states and territories were taken over by Islam, which of course led to the movement known as the Crusades: the often very sincere, but ill-fated attempts by Christians to take back once holy land, but now Islamic-controlled territory. The 11th and 12th centuries were dark and bloody, a real low point for the church capped by the fact that Europe came under almost complete control by the Roman Catholic church. And the head of that Roman church is of course the Pope, who was given power to authenticate, to validate, to administer, to dispense spiritual power. As they would say, "One man in control."

The pope and the church enforced itself on the state. Kings and popes clash with each other, all for the sake of power. When the church has that kind of power it feeds something very carnal in man which leads to more corruption. Because when your interests are all focused on the state, your spiritual concerns tend to fade away. The more that we are concerned with things going on outside of the church, the more it affects our interests inside the church. There is nothing new under the sun. And that is exactly what happened during this time. The church became about territory, power, and prestige.

To give an illustration of how low things got in this period, we have events like the Papal Schism. Three men were vying for power, each one saying that they were the real pope. Historians laugh at such a thing today, because it *is* laughable. They were thirsty not for the spiritual seat, but for power and the right to rule. Things were dark, indeed. It may have seemed like the true church had vanished altogether, but we know truth never dies, nor does darkness last.

In fact, it was the Reformers that reminded us of this truth. There was a phrase that became the cry of the reformers: "Post Tenebras Lux," meaning, "After darkness, light." That wonderful battle cry takes us now to the forerunners of the Reformation.

The Forerunners (12th-15th century)
In the middle of all that darkness, there were flickers, glimmers, spots on horizon, showing that God's truth never dies. We can talk of many forerunners to the Reformation, but there are three of note:

Waldensians (1184-1500s)

The first were the Waldensians, named after Peter Waldo who was born in 1140 in Southern France. The one thing we need to know about Peter Waldo was that he was very wealthy. He had lots of money, but no happiness. And yet his soul was provoked, and he tried to turn to the Word of God for answers. But there was one problem. He wanted God's Word, but he couldn't get a Bible because at the time, the Bible was written in Latin and very inaccessible. However, since he was rich, he was able to hire two Latin scholars to translate the Latin Vulgate for him. And something amazing happened: his life was transformed. In fact, his life was *reformed* as he started to read the Bible in his own language. *He turned from material wealth to spiritual wealth.* The more he read, the more he proclaimed what he was reading, and of course the Roman Catholic church did not like that one bit. In fact, in 1184 they excommunicated him. The Waldensians, the movement of those who followed his example, were declared heretics. However, that attempt by Rome to stamp out a *Scripture alone* movement, would not succeed as the Waldensians endured in the centuries that followed and paved the way for other forerunners.

John Wycliffe (1329-1384)

John Wycliffe has been dubbed "The Morningstar of the Reformation", because of how he helped pave the way for the Reformers. Wycliffe was a scholar at Oxford, who himself knew Latin, and as he observed the corrupt religious leaders of his day, it drove him to Word. As he observed what was going on around him, he saw the growing disconnect between what was going on in the church and what God was saying in His Word. And so he undertook a translation of his own. He believed that the people needed to see what God has said, about Himself, about how to live.

Waldo and Wycliffe both believed strongly in *Scripture alone,* in the authority of the Bible, which meant rejecting papal misuse and abuse. He wrote a paper strongly against the office of the pope. And we can thank Wycliffe for a number of other unbiblical practices being exposed: baptismal regeneration, indulgences, and so on.

John Hus (1373-1415)

Around the same time, in Bohemia (modern-day Czech Republic), John Hus was inspired by what he heard was going on in England through the work of Wycliffe. He was driven to the Word, and he too started acting on what he was reading. Hus also saw the disconnect between what the Bible said and what the church was practicing. But Hus, unlike those before him, was also an accomplished preacher, and he started preaching truths such as:

1) Christ is the true head of the Church, not the pope (*Christ alone*).

2) Christ's people are to sing, because it's in God's Word (Eph. 5:19). At that point, people were condemned for singing.

Eventually, he was invited to the Council of Constance in 1414, thinking that they were interested in discussing his reforms. When he arrived, they turned on him. They tied him to a stake, and legend says that as he burned, he sung a hymn. The scandal of it all, that he was singing. Legend also says that he said this: "You cook a goose now (his name, "Hus," means goose) but in 100 years, God will raise a swan…" And indeed, God would provide Martin Luther, whose symbol became the swan. The spark indeed had been lit, the way had been paved. The Reformation was coming...but reformation had long since begun.

The Reformation (16th century)
Look at how much happened before we even come to the Reformation. I pray you see that it didn't just happen as an isolated event. But let us talk about the key components of the 16th century. Many of us know the context of Martin Luther's life. But setting the table for Luther, was a man by the name of Erasmus.

Erasmus (1466–1536)
Erasmus was a Dutch scholar of the highest order, and a humanist. That word doesn't mean what it means today; it meant a raw product of the Renaissance. The battle cry of the Renaissance was *Ad Fontes*: back to the source. So what did Erasmus do? He took his Vulgate and said, "This is not enough. I need to know the Greek words that God inspired. Erasmus toured all around Europe gathering as many Greek manuscripts as he could. His actions were unheard of at the time. There was no collection of Greek manuscripts gathered into one New Testament. But Erasmus did just that, and in 1518, he published the Novem Testamentum (the New Testament). This was a profound moment in the history of God's church. They had never had access to a full New Testament. And of course, this coincided with the timing of the printing press, Gutenberg's invention. Erasmus put that Greek New Testament in the printing press and the next thing you know, it was all over Europe.

Of course, this Greek New Testament made its way into the hands of a certain German monk. While he was holed up in a castle, he translated that Greek into German. And that

German Bible spread throughout Germany. Reformation was now a fire, spreading to men like Ulrich Zwingli...

Ulrich Zwingli (1484-1531)
Zwingli was a pastor in Zurich, Switzerland. On his first day in the pulpit, he started preaching in Matthew 1 and preached through the entire New Testament over six years, verse by verse. He took Zurich by storm; they had never heard anything like that at all. Also in Switzerland...

John Calvin (1509-1564)
Then there was Calvin, a pastor in Geneva, Switzerland with a brilliant mind. Calvin's greatest contribution to the Reformation is his *Institutes of the Christian Religion*. Every other systematic theology of the time was based on tradition, on man's opinions. John Calvin went straight to the Word of God, which is what the Reformation was, and is, all about.

Other Reformers
These men in turn inspired others, like John Knox. Knox sat under Calvin, and took his "back to the Bible" teaching to Scotland and reformed a whole country. There was William Tyndale in England, and the list goes on and on. When you think of the Reformation impacting Europe and England, what about those Puritans that established the New World while seeking originally, first and foremost, the freedom to get back to the Bible, to be pure and stand on Biblical truth. And on and on it goes. We stand in the line of Reformers. As history continues, we are always being reformed. As we consider that, we close and revisit our three questions:

When did the Reformation Begin? Was it in 1517? No. That was a huge moment, and God used it as a catapult, but it started long before that. In fact, after a look at history, it becomes clear that from the moment God decided to use imperfect people to build His church, reformation was needed. Christ is making that bride spotless through reformation.

What was the main issue of the Reformation? Of course, many would say *justification by faith alone*, and indeed that's a great plank. Faith alone, that's an important tenet. However, there was an even greater issue going on in the background, and that was authority. Who has the authority? Is it a three-prong stool or is it one? As far as the reformation was concerned, *the* main issue was *Scripture alone*.

What famous writings sparked the Reformation? Luther's 95 Theses? No, God's Word in the hands of God's people in their own languages. It was access to God's Word, reading it, seeing it, that sparked the Reformation. And we leave the last word to Luther:

> I opposed indulgences and all papists, but never by force. I simply taught, preached, wrote God's Word: otherwise I did nothing. And then, while I slept or drank the Word so greatly weakened the papacy that never a prince or emperor did such damage to it. I did nothing: the Word did it all.[3]

---

[3] Stephen Nichols, *The Reformation: How a Monk and a Mallet Changed the World,* (Wheaton, IL: Crossway, 2007), 38.

That continues to be the case today when we see true reform. It is the Word that does the work. It's always been forming us, and we are the ones that need reforming. As the Word changes us, may we cling to those five solas as the history of God's church continues.

2

SCRIPTURE ALONE

Derek Green

The year was 1515. Pope Leo X needed money for the completion of St. Peter's Basilica, and Albert of Mainz wanted another title.[1] At only 24 year of age, Albert was already the archbishop of Magdeburg and the administrator of the Archdiocese of Halberstadt, and now he wanted the Archbishopric of Mainz as well. But there was a problem: canon law prevented the accumulation of offices without a dispensation from the Pope.

And so a plan was hatched. For a fee—a large fee—Pope Leo would grant Albert his dispensation, making it possible for Albert to acquire his third title. Albert would have to borrow the money, but that wasn't a problem because the Pope would allow Albert's monk, Johann Tetzel, to raise the funds to pay back the debt through a special sale of

---

[1] Stephen J. Nichols, *Martin Luther's Ninety-Five Theses* (Phillipsburg, NJ: P&R Publishing, 2002), 11.

indulgences.[2] Some of the profits would go toward St. Peter's Basilica, and some would go toward retiring Albert's debt.

Catholic teaching made a distinction between the guilt that sin incurs and the penalty that has to be paid. Even though the guilt of believer's sin may be forgiven, there still remains temporal punishment for that sin which the sinner himself must pay.[3] In this life, doing penance (prayer, fasting, almsgiving, works of mercy and patient suffering) remits temporal punishment. If a believer dies in Christ before that temporal punishment is complete, the balance is paid in Purgatory, where a believer is purified through suffering and made fit for entrance into the Kingdom of Heaven. The church also taught that a believer's temporal punishment in this life could be reduced through the acquisition of indulgences, which were dispensed by the church to penitent sinners under certain conditions.

Indulgences were drawn from the Treasury of Merit, which the church understood to be "a storehouse of grace which was accumulated by the meritorious work of Christ and by the superabundant merit of the saints."[4] This "storehouse of grace" was at the church's disposal. It had been filled by the righteous work of Christ and by the good works of the saints, and the church had access to this "storehouse," and the authority to dispense the grace within it to repentant

---

[2] Hans Hillerbrand, *The Division of Christendom: Christianity I the Sixteenth Century* (Louisville, KY: Westminster John Knox Press, 2007), 35.

[3] The *Catechism of the Catholic Church:* Sec. 1472 and 1473: http://www.vatican.va/archive/ENG0015/_P4G.HTM.

[4] Michael Kruger, *Canon Revisited* (Wheaton, IL: Crossway, 2012), 34.

sinners. The sinner would then be absolved of some or all of their temporal punishments for sin in this life.

In the case of Tetzel, Rome agreed to allow the sale of a unique indulgence that would return the sinner to a state of innocence. You could even buy one for a loved already in purgatory.[5]

Going from town to town, Tetzel would lay it on thick, crying something like: "Listen to the voices of your dear dead relatives and friends, beseeching you and saying, 'Pity us, pity us. We are in dire torment from which you can redeem us for a pittance... Will you let us lie here in flames? Will you delay our promised glory?" And then his familiar little jingle, as cruel as it is heretical: "as soon as the coin in the coffer rings, the soul from purgatory springs."[6] By 1517, Martin Luther had had enough. Luther would later write of Tetzel:

> With might and main he sold grace for money as dearly or as cheaply as he could." You could even purchase indulgences for future sins. Luther recorded one incident: "After Tetzel had received a substantial amount of money at Leipzig, a nobleman asked him if it were possible to receive a letter of indulgence for a future sin. Tetzel quickly answered in the affirmative, insisting, however, that the payment had to made at once. This the nobleman did, receiving there-upon a letter and seal from Tetzel. When Tetzel left Leipzig the nobleman attacked him along the way, gave him a thorough beating, and sent

---

[5] Matthew Barrett, *God's Word Alone: The Authority of Scripture* (Grand Rapids, IL: Zondervan, 2016), 35.

[6] John Tetzel, "A Sermon [1517]," in Hans J. Hillerbrand, ed. *The Protestant Reformation* (New York: Harper Perennial, 2009) 19–21.

him back empty-handed to Leipzig, saying that this was the future sin he had in mind.[7]

On October 31 of 1517, what's come to be known as "Reformation Day," Martin Luther, who was then an Augustinian Monk living in Wittenberg, Germany and teaching at the University, mailed a letter to Albert, who was now the Archbishop of Mainz, complaining about Tetzel's abuses,[8] and he posted a list of 95 points for discussion on the door of the Castle Church in Wittenberg. It was titled "*Disputation of Martin Luther on the Power and Efficacy of Indulgences.*" He posted it in Latin instead of German because it wasn't meant for public consumption but to invite academic and theological discussion. Specifically, Luther wanted to talk about indulgences and the limits of papal authority. Did the Pope really have power over purgatory? Did the Pope really have authority for the forgiveness of sins and the remission of their penalty?

The debate Luther wanted never happened. In the providence of God, Johannes Gutenberg had created the printing press some 70 years earlier, and in January 1518 some students at the University translated Luther's disputation from Latin into German, printed copies, and began distributing them. It's said that within two weeks, copies of Luther's 95 theses had spread across Germany. Within two months copies had spread across Europe.

---

[7] Andreas Malessa, *The Unreformed Martin Luther: A Serious (and Not So Serious) Look at the Man Behind the Myths* (Grand Rapids: Kregel Publications, 2017), 28.

[8] *The Works of Martin Luther*. Ed. and trans. Adolph Spaeth, L.D. Reed, Henry Eyster Jacobs, et al. (Philadelphia: A. J. Holman Company, 1915), Vol. 1, 25–28.

Rome's response was decisive. Tetzel responded by calling Luther a heretic and demanding his execution by burning.[9] The Pope appointed a theologian named Sylvester Prierias to respond to Luther, and Prierias saw that the root issue behind Luther's challenge was the issue of authority. In his response, he wrote the following:

> He who does not accept the doctrine of the Church of Rome and the pontiff of Rome as an infallible rule of faith, from which the Holy Scriptures, too, draw their strength and authority, is a heretic.[10]

Mark the language. Prierias wasn't simply saying that the doctrine of the Church of Rome and of the Pope were infallible. He was saying something far more insidious. He was saying that the doctrine of the Church of Rome and of the Pope *are the source* from which the Scriptures themselves "draw their strength and authority."

This question of authority was central to the schism between the reformers and the Roman church, and it's at the very heart of the doctrine of Sola Scriptura. The official teaching office of the Catholic Church is called the Magisterium. The Magisterium is composed primarily of the Pope and his Bishops,[11] and the Magisterium has authority to interpret the Scriptures and to establish official church teaching. This is because in the Magisterium, the Catholic Church sees an unbroken succession all the way back to Peter

---

[9] Michael Reeves, *The Unquenchable Flame: Discovering the Heart of the Reformation* (Nashville: B&H Academic, 2010), 44.

[10] Quoted in Heiko A. Oberman, *Luther: Man between God and the Devil* (New Haven: Yale University Press, 1982), 198.

[11] Kruger, *Canon Revisited*, 39.

and the apostles. According to Dei Verbum, the Second Vatican Council's Dogmatic Constitution on Divine Revelation, "*the Apostles left bishops as their successors, "handing over" to them "the authority to teach in their own place."*"[12] It should be noted that Dei Verbum is a recent document, ratified under Pope Paul VI on November 18, 1965. However, in this instance, it articulates beliefs that were well established in the Roman Catholic Church in Luther's day as well.

For the Catholic Church, ultimate authority comes from three sources: Scripture, tradition, and the Magisterium. According to Dei Verbum, these three "*are so linked and joined together that one cannot stand without the others.*"[13] Clearly, any claim that Scripture "*cannot stand*" without tradition is problematic, to put it mildly. However, Dei Verbum goes further: "(it is) through the same tradition that the Church's full canon of the sacred books is known,"[14] and further, that "the task of authentically interpreting the word of God, whether written or handed on, has been entrusted exclusively to the living teaching office of the Church."[15]

Think about what this is saying. Although the Magisterium is only one of three sources of authority for the Catholic Church—Scripture and tradition being the other two—Dei Verbum says that it's the Magisterium that has the exclusive authority to decide which writings are even

---

[12] See http://www.vatican.va/archive/hist_councils/ii_vatican_council/documents/vat-ii_const_19651118_dei-verbum_en.html Section II:7, accessed on October 26, 2017.

[13] Ibid, Section 2:10, accessed on October 26, 2017.

[14] Ibid, Section 2:8(c), accessed on October 26, 2017.

[15] Ibid, Section 2:10, accessed on October 26, 2017.

classified as Scripture to begin with, and then the authority to interpret those writings for the church.[16]

Cardinal Hosius, papal legate to the Council of Trent in the mid 1500s, took all the pretense out and put it like this *"The Scriptures have only as much force as the fables of Aesop, if destitute of the authority of the church."*[17] In other words, the Scriptures have no authority over us whatsoever unless the Magisterium says they do, because they don't become "Scripture" until the Magisterium says they are. Karl Rahner put it even more bluntly: "[Scripture] exists because the church exists."[18]

For the reformers, this was unbearable. In Calvin's *Institutes of the Christian Religion*, he wrote "A most pernicious error widely prevails that the Scripture has only so much weight as is conceded to it by the consent of the church. As if the eternal and inviolable truth of God depended upon the decision of men!"[19]

The problem of course is that there can be only one ultimate authority. Rome can say that ultimate authority lies in Scripture, tradition, and the Magisterium—which is wrong in and of itself—but if the Magisterium has authority to decide what is Scripture and what isn't, and then it has authority to decide how that Scripture should be interpreted

---

[16] Kruger, *Canon Revisited*, 39.

[17] Confutatio Brentii, "Opera", 1.530. English trans. from Francis Turretin, *Institutes of Elenctic Theology*, trans. George Musgrave Giger, ed. James T. Dennison Jr., 3 vols. (Phillipsburg, NJ: P&R, 1992-1997), 1:86 (2.6.2).

[18] Karl Rahner, *Foundations of Christian Faith: An Introduction to the Idea of Christianity* (New York: Crossroad, 1997), 362.

[19] John Calvin, *Institutes of the Christian Religion* in *The Library of Christian Classics: Vol. XX-XXI*, ed. John T. McNeill, trans. Ford Lewis Battles (Philadelphia: Westminster, 1960), 1.VII.1.

and how it should be applied, we must ask the question of who the ultimate authority really is. Is it the Word of God, or is it the opinion of men?

Well, back to Sylvester Prierias. Prierias had written that "He who does not accept the doctrine of the Church of Rome and the pontiff of Rome as an infallible rule of faith, from which the Holy Scriptures, too, draw their strength and authority, is a heretic" Luther responded by pointing out that Prierias had quoted no Scripture in defending his position and that in fact the Papacy could not be inerrant because it had contradicted itself on a number of occasions.[20]

Luther was now on record stating that the Pope could err. To be clear, Rome does not believe that the Pope is infallible at all times, but only when he speaks "from the chair," or in Latin, "*ex cathedra,*" in his capacity as the Vicar of Christ on earth. Prierias was ahead of his time in one way, because the doctrine of Papal infallibility was not officially adopted by the Catholic Church until the First Vatican Council under Pius IX in 1870.[21] But just as in the issue of authority as set forth in

---

[20] Matthew Barrett, *God's Word Alone,* 36–37.

[21] "We *teach and define* as a divinely revealed dogma that when the Roman pontiff speaks EX CATHEDRA, that is, when, in the exercise of his office as shepherd and teacher of all Christians, in virtue of his supreme apostolic authority, he defines a doctrine concerning faith or morals to be held by the whole church, he possesses, by the divine assistance promised to him in blessed Peter, that infallibility which the divine Redeemer willed his church to enjoy in defining doctrine concerning faith or morals. *Therefore*, such definitions of the Roman pontiff are of themselves, and not by the consent of the church, irreformable. So then, should anyone, which God forbid, have the temerity to reject this definition of ours: let him be anathema." Decrees of the First Vatican Council. Canons, Session 4, paragraph 4, section 9. http://www.papalencyclicals.net/Councils/ecum

Dei Verbum, the seeds of the dogma were fairly entrenched even by Luther's day,[22] and in 1870, Rome simply adopted officially what had already been believed for many years.

The following year Luther was examined by Cardinal Cajetan in Augsburg. Cajetan knew that the root issue was the question of authority, and brought up *Unigenitus*, a papal bull from 1343, in which Pope Clement VI had declared that the merits of Christ are a treasure of indulgences. Cajetan said that Luther's problem was that he didn't believe the Pope.[23]

Luther responded by saying that he would not reject the clear teaching of Scripture in favor of a decree from a fallible human pope. Cajetan reminded Luther that the Pope was the interpreter of Scripture. Luther replied, "His Holiness abuses Scripture. I deny that he is above Scripture."[24] Again, Luther goes on record stating that the Pope could err.

In 1519, Luther met Johann Eck for a debate in Leipzig, and Eck immediately steered the debate toward the issue of authority. Luther said that Christ, not the Pope, was the Head of the Church, and he defended it from Scripture. In what was clearly a trap, Eck replied by saying that if Luther refused to acknowledge the Pope as head over the church, he must be in league with Jan (John) Hus, whom Rome had condemned and burned as a heretic for the same reason,

---

20.htm (accessed Nov. 11, 2017).

[22] https://en.wikipedia.org/wiki/Papal_infallibility (accessed on October 26, 2017).

[23] R.C. Sproul, *Scripture Alone: The Evangelical Doctrine* (Phillipsburg, NJ:P&R Publishing, 2013), 16. See also Roland Bainton, *Here I Stand: A Life of Martin Luther* (New York: Abingdon Press, 1950) 94.

[24] Matthew Barrett, *God's Word Alone*, 38.

some 100 years earlier at the Council of Constance. [25] Luther admitted that he was in agreement with Hus on this issue and said that the Council of Constance was wrong in condemning him. He said,

> I assert that a council has sometimes erred and may sometimes err. Nor has a council authority to establish new articles of faith. A council cannot make divine right out of that which by nature is not divine right. Councils have contradicted each other, for the recent Lateran Council has reversed the claim of the councils of Constance and Basel that a council is above a pope. A simple layman armed with Scripture is to be believed above a pope or a council without it. As for the pope's decretal on indulgences I say that neither the Church nor the pope can establish articles of faith. These must come from Scripture. For the sake of Scripture we should reject pope and councils.[26]

So now Luther was on record saying that the Pope can be and has been wrong, church counsels can be and have been wrong, and church teaching can be and has been wrong. Scripture *alone*, Luther said, is inerrant and therefore Scripture *alone* is our final authority in all matters of religion. For Luther and the reformers, the authority of Scripture flowed from the inspiration and inerrancy of Scripture. Scripture *alone* is inerrant because Scripture *alone* is inspired

---

[25] http://www.papalencyclicals.net/councils/ecum16.htm (accessed on October 26, 2017).
[26] Matthew Barrett, *God's Word Alone,* 103.

by God. And because Scripture *alone* is inspired and inerrant, Scripture *alone* is our final authority. Popes, church councils, church teachings, traditions, and everything else are fallible, therefore they are *subservient*—they are *under* the authority of Scripture.

The following year, the Pope issued a papal bull stating that Luther's books were to be burned, and that Luther would be anathematized in 60 days if he failed to recant. When he received the bull, Luther burned it publicly, and the following month, January 1521, he was excommunicated by the Roman Catholic Church.[27]

In April 1521, Luther was summoned to Worms to appear before Charles V, ruler of the Holy Roman Empire, for an Imperial Diet."[28] Luther was told to recant of his teachings. Luther's reply the following day is famous:

> Unless I am convinced by the testimony of the Scriptures or by clear reason (for I do not trust either in the pope or in councils alone, since it is well known that they often err and contradict themselves), I am bound by the Scriptures I have quoted and my conscience is captive to the Word of God. I cannot and I will not retract anything, since it is neither safe nor right to go against conscience. I cannot do otherwise, here I stand, may God help me, Amen.[29]

Within days, Charles V had issued the Edict of Worms, declaring Martin Luther to be an outlaw and criminal, making

---

[27] Matthew Barrett, *God's Word Alone*, 43.
[28] Matthew Barrett, *God's Word Alone*, 43.
[29] Matthew Barrett, *God's Word Alone*, 45.

it illegal to own his writings, and ordering Luther's books to be burned.[30] To protect his life, Luther's friends staged his kidnapping and whisked him away to Wartburg Castle where he translated the New Testament into the German language.

The Doctrine of Sola Scriptura

With that context in place, let's examine the doctrine of Sola Scriptura more closely. We'll clarify what we mean when we say "Sola Scriptura." What does it mean, and what doesn't it mean? Secondly, we'll consider the doctrine of Sola Scriptura under the headings of inspiration, inerrancy, clarity, and sufficiency. Thirdly, we'll look at how the doctrine of Sola Scriptura worked itself out in the preaching ministries of the reformers. And fourthly, we'll consider why this is so important in our day.

Sola Scriptura defined

Matthew Barrett offers a simple but clear definition:

> Sola Scriptura means that only Scripture, because it is God's inspired Word, is our inerrant, sufficient, and final authority for the church.[31]

Central to the debate in the reformation was the connection between inspiration, inerrancy and authority. God's Word is inerrant because it is inspired–because it comes from God Himself. And its inspiration and inerrancy, in turn, are the basis of its authority. Why is the Word of God

---

[30] http://www.crivoice.org/creededictworms.html (accessed Nov. 7, 2017).

[31] Matthew Barrett, *God's Word Alone*, 333.

the *final* authority for the church? The Word of God is the *final* authority for the church because the Word of God is inspired, and because by virtue of its inspiration, the Word of God is inerrant.

That's what Sola Scriptura means. What doesn't it mean? Sola Scriptura doesn't mean that Scripture is the *only* authority for the church. The reformers valued Biblical church government, and they valued church councils and church history and the teachings of the church fathers. But here's the difference: when there was a conflict, Scripture reigned supreme. Scripture alone is inspired, therefore Scripture alone is inerrant, therefore Scripture alone is the *final* authority for the church.

Inspiration, Inerrancy, Clarity, and Sufficiency
Inspiration
What do we mean when we say that Scripture is "inspired by God?" We mean that God, by His Spirit, while preserving the style and individuality of the human authors of Scripture, caused them to write precisely what God intended, with the result that the author's words are the very words of God and are therefore authoritative, inerrant, and sure.[32] "All Scripture is breathed out by God and profitable for teaching, for reproof, for correction, and for training in righteousness, that the man of God may be complete, equipped for every good work" (2 Tim. 3:16–17).

For the reformers, everything could be reduced to one foundational, awe-inspiring truth: God had spoken! Just think of it! Free access to the Scriptures is something we take for

---

[32] Adapted from Matthew Barrett's definition. Matthew Barrett, *God's Word Alone*, 229.

granted, but put yourself in the shoes of a European commoner in the early 1500s. The Word of God has been, by and large, held captive in the Latin of the Roman Catholic Church for a thousand years, and now it seems that God is doing a work and there's a chance that you could actually have a fragment or book of the Bible - or dare to dream - maybe even a whole Bible in your own language. What would that mean! Men, women, children, entire families, counting the cost and paying the price, so many of them losing their lives. They knew the risk, but *God had spoken,* and they had to know what He had said. Oh, that we would recover the wonder of this truth in our day: God has spoken!

In the Old Testament, "God spoke through the prophets at many times and in many ways." And He didn't only "speak" through them—He caused His Words to be written down. Jesus believed the Old Testament was inspired. He often referred to OT writings as "Scripture" from God. The apostle Peter wrote that "no prophecy was ever produced by the will of man, but men spoke from God as they were carried along by the Holy Spirit" (2 Peter 1:21).

What about New Testament writings? In 1 Thess. 2:13, Paul wrote "And we also thank God constantly for this, that when you received the word of God, which you heard from us, you accepted it not as the word of men but as what is really is, the word of God."

Verbal, plenary inspiration simply states that every single individual word of Scripture, in the original language, is inspired by God, and therefore the entire Bible, in all of its individual parts, is authoritative. In fact, R.C. Sproul said that "Jesus didn't just believe in plenary inspiration, or even verbal inspiration. Jesus' view of Scripture was "jot and tittle" inspiration. Not just every word... not just every letter...but every vowel point. Every comma. Every period was inspired by the Holy Spirit so that not one word of Scripture can possibly fail."[33]

And because Scripture is God's Word, it comes to us with divine authority. Calvin wrote that "we owe to the Scripture the same reverence which we owe to God; because it has proceeded from him alone, and has nothing belonging to man mixed with it."*[34]* The authority of Scripture flows from its inspiration.

Inerrancy

Inerrancy simply says that Scripture, in the original writings, never errs in anything that the Biblical authors say.[35]

The "core idea" behind the doctrine of inerrancy is, "Scripture is trustworthy because the God behind Scripture is trustworthy."[36] The inspired Scriptures come from God, and because they come from God they reflect the character of God. And God is true, therefore as Proverbs 30:5 says, "every word of God proves true."

Matthew Barrett writes,

---

[33] R.C. Sproul, in a sermon on Luke 16:17. See http://renewingyourmind.org/2014/10/31/scripture-the-formal-cause-of-the-reformation referenced at 19:00.

[34] Calvin, John. Calvin's Commentaries, *"The Epistles to Timothy, Titus, and Philemon,"* trans. from the original Latin. Rev. William Pringle (Christian Classics Ethereal Library: http://www.ccel.org) excerpted from commentary on 2 Timothy 3:16. http://www.ccel.org/ccel/calvin/calcom43.iv.iv.iii.html.

[35] Adapted from Matthew Barrett's definition. Barrett, 264.

[36] Carl Trueman, "The God of Unconditional Promise," in *The Trustworthiness of God: Perspectives on the Nature of Scripture,* ed. Paul Helm and Carl R. Trueman (Grand Rapids: Eerdmans, 2002), 178.

countless times we read that the Lord is the "true God." The same is said of Christ, the Son of God, who is full of grace and truth, bears witness to the truth, speaks the truth, and is himself the truth. The Holy Spirit is referred to as the "Spirit of truth" and is identified as the one "who is the truth." There is a Trinitarian nature to truth, for Father, Son, and Holy Spirit are the one true God who speaks words of truth.[37]

Like we've already said, the inerrancy of Scripture is directly connected with Sola Scriptura. The reformers did not despise church councils. In fact, they approved of them and often quoted them in their writings. Where they broke from Rome was in the amount of authority they allowed them. Because church councils, tradition, and even Popes could err, they could not occupy the same level of authority as the Scriptures. As Luther said, "But everyone, indeed, knows that at times (the fathers) have erred as men will; therefore, I am ready to trust them only when they prove their opinions from Scripture, which has never erred."[38]

Clarity

For centuries, the Catholic Church had argued that Scripture was too complicated, too difficult, and too murky to be understood by the common man. The claim was simple: if Scripture gets into the hands of the common man, the common woman, the common child, and everyone were to interpret its meaning for themselves, there's no counting the

---

[37] Matthew Barrett, *God's Word Alone*, 273.
[38] Matthew Barrett, *God's Word Alone*, 289.

heresies that could result. Thus, Scripture must remain in the possession of the church. The church must interpret the Scriptures for the people, because they are not equipped to interpret it for themselves.

The reformers didn't deny that this could happen, and church history bears witness to the fact that this did happen—frequently. But the reformers also said that while this could and probably would happen, it was no justification for keeping the Word of God under lock and key. Every individual should have access to the Scriptures. But with privilege comes responsibility. We are responsible before God to seek a right understanding of His Word so that we can apply it rightly in our lives.

The clarity of Scripture means exactly what it says it means. God has spoken, and He has spoken clearly. God has spoken to us in the languages of men. He condescended to speak in ways that were culturally sensitive. Think of all the agrarian imagery Jesus used in his parables because He was speaking with a people familiar with agriculture. God has spoken to us in different genres: history, psalms, poetry, wisdom literature, epistles, doctrinal treatise, apocalyptic literature, appealing not just to the mind, but to the heart, the will, and the imagination. And God has spoken to us in His Son! In the Old Testament, God would deliver his message through a prophet, but in Christ God has come to deliver His message Himself. Jesus' representation of the character of God, for anyone who had eyes to see, was so clear that He could say to Philip, "if you have seen me, you have seen the Father" (John 14:9).

But now two qualifiers. Firstly, God has spoken clearly, but that doesn't mean that Scripture is always easy and never difficult. There are difficult passages to be sure. But what do we do when we encounter a difficult passage in the Bible? We use the Bible to interpret it! We use the clearer passages in the Bible to help us understand the difficult ones.

Secondly: God has spoken clearly, but doesn't mean we can come to a full sense of the true meaning of Scripture by reason alone. We are fallen, and we desperately need of the illuminating work of the Spirit of God if we are ever going to come to a true understanding of Scripture. "The natural person does not accept the things of the Spirit of God, for they are folly to him, and he is not able to understand them because they are spiritually discerned" (1 Cor 2:14). The inability of fallen man to fully understand and accept the full meaning and spiritual weight of the Word of God is not because His Word is unclear. It's because our minds are unclear. Paul wrote in 2 Cor 4: "And even if our gospel is veiled, it is veiled to those who are perishing. In their case the god of this world has blinded the minds of the unbelievers, to keep them from seeing the light of the gospel of the glory of Christ, who is the image of God. For what we proclaim is not ourselves, but Jesus Christ as Lord, with ourselves as your servants for Jesus' sake. For God, who said, 'Let light shine out of darkness,' has shone in our hearts to give the light of the knowledge of the glory of God in the face of Jesus Christ."

Word and Spirit, then, have always gone together. The Spirit was active with the Word in Creation. The Spirit was active with the Word in the inspiration. The Spirit was active with the Word in incarnation. And in the present, the Spirit is active with the Word in regeneration and in sanctification.

Sufficiency

As we saw earlier, Rome located ultimate authority in three places: Scripture, tradition, and the Magisterium. The reformers, however, located ultimate authority in Scripture alone. Only Scripture is inspired, therefore only Scripture is infallible. And because Scripture alone is infallible, and because it is clear, Scripture alone is sufficient for faith and practice.

In Deuteronomy 4, God says "And now, O Israel, listen to the statutes and the rules that I am teaching you, and do them, that you may live, and go in and take possession of the land that the LORD, the God of your fathers, is giving you. You shall not add to the word that I command you, nor take from it, that you may keep the commandments of the LORD your God that I command you."

Israel is preparing to cross the Jordan to take possession of the land, and God is preparing them by rehearsing with them the principles by which they were to live, the blessings that would flow from obedience, and the curses that would result from disobedience. God's instruction was all they needed to know in order to know how to live when they took possession of the land. God had told them *all* they needed to know—"you shall not add to the Word that I command you." And they needed to know *all of it*—"you shall not take away from it." Simply put, God's Word was (and is) sufficient.

In the New Testament, Paul wrote in 2 Timothy, "all Scripture is breathed out by God and profitable for teaching, for reproof, for correction, and for training in righteousness, that the man of God may be complete, equipped for every good work." Again I'll quote Matthew Barrett because he says it so well, "Scripture is not merely helpful but is the source we turn to for all of life as a Christian. Anything God would call us to do in obedience to his will as his children can be found in Scripture. Scripture teaches, reproves, corrects, and even trains us in righteousness. Those who follow God follow Scripture and find that Scripture will instruct them in living a godly life."[39]

In the Preaching Ministries of the Reformers

Church historian R.L. Dabney wrote the Reformation reversed "the customary disuse of the divinely-appointed ordinance of preaching."[40] He wrote "the Great Reformation was emphatically a revival of gospel preaching. All the leading Reformers, whether in Germany, Switzerland, England, or Scotland, were constant preachers, and their sermons were prevalently expository."[41]

This is because they understood that Scripture is more than just a book for the church. God has spoken. He has spoken to us in His Word, and He has spoken to us in His Son! By the inspiration of His Spirit, God has given to us an inerrant, clear, and sufficient Word, and our *greatest need* is to know what He has said. And it is through His Word that the Spirit brings light to understand it and power to walk it in. The Word of God is the voice of God to the soul of a believer. As a result, the preaching ministries of the reformers were marked primarily by *expositional* preaching. Preaching through Scripture, line by line, chapter by chapter, book by book, because they knew that the people's greatest need was to hear the Word of God.

---

[39] Matthew Barrett, *God's Word Alone*, 342.

[40] R.L. Dabney, *Sacred Rhetoric: A Course of Lectures on Preaching* (Richmond: Presbyterian Committee of Publication, 1870), 345.

[41] R.L. Dabney, *Sacred Rhetoric*, 26.

Importance for Today

The Reformers differentiated between the *formal* cause of the Reformation and the *material* cause of the Reformation. The material cause is the root issue. It's the essence of the debate. The material cause of the Reformation was Sola Fide— Justification by faith alone. But the formal cause—the "*form*" or "*shape*" that gave structure to the debate, at least at first, was Sola Scriptura. And it *had* to be! If Sola Scriptura isn't true, then anything goes, and we'll never know if we have justification right. But if Sola Scriptura is true, then Scripture alone teaches us about justification. And Scripture teaches us that we are justified by grace alone through faith alone in Christ alone to the glory of God alone. This is why this is so important for *our* day. Our position on Sola Scriptura will determine our position on all of these other doctrines.

The Catholic Church's location of undue authority in their teaching offices and official tradition is but one example of the ongoing impulse in a fallen world to dilute and diminish the supremacy of God's Word. Behind this impulse is Satan himself, who says to every generation and in every culture, "has God really said?"

Today, one of the ways this challenge comes to us is in the form of existentialism. We may reject the notion that church tradition has the same authority as Scripture, but then we turn around and base our decisions on feeling, on emotion, on experience. We're simply replacing "I know what the Bible says, but church tradition tells me..." with "I know what the Bible says, but my feelings are telling me..." As products of our age, we're simply changing one of the variables in the equation, elevating emotionalism and personal experience to the level of Scripture, instead of church tradition.

Instead of changing the variables, we need to rethink the math. As Jim Elliot once said, addressing a very similar issue, "why do you need a voice, when you have a verse?" The authority of the Word of God is peerless. It is ultimate. Again to quote John Calvin, "we owe to the Scripture the same reverence which we owe to God; because it has proceeded from him alone, and has nothing belonging to man mixed with it."

3

CHRIST ALONE

Josh Anderson

Explaining why we believe that salvation is through Christ alone in one chapter is a little bit like preaching the whole Bible in 40 minutes—you can only attempt to scratch the surface. My hope for you in the wake of this chapter is that when you put your head on your pillow to sleep tonight, when you wake up tomorrow morning, whether you are at work or school or home, whether you are young or old, when you are victorious in fleeing from temptation and when you fail and choose to sin; that in this midst of all of those things you would be absolutely confident that God loves you and is for you because of the unique glory of his Son and your Saviour, Jesus Christ.

The doctrine of salvation through Christ alone is not a doctrine that constrains us; it doesn't keep us from something better or more certain. It frees us to put our full weight on Jesus and find that God is unshakably and eternally for us. That's where we're heading.

Only President Nixon Could Go To China
In 1972, the United States president Richard Nixon made a historic diplomatic trip to communist China. The two countries had been estranged for many years, and the strongly anti-communist feelings both among the US government and public made any such trip seem like political suicide. But Nixon made the trip, beginning the process of thawing U.S-Chinese relations without suffering any significant political fallout. Any "soft-on-communism" charge that the Democrats might have leveled against him wouldn't stick because Nixon's anti-communist credentials both personally and politically were so airtight. The Democratic leader of the Senate said this of Nixon in an interview at the time: "Only a Republican, perhaps only a Nixon, could have made this break and gotten away with it." Nixon's identity and his political work made it possible for him to bridge the gap between the US and China in a way that no other politician could. Only Nixon could go to China. He was uniquely suited to the task.

When we say that our salvation is through Christ alone, we mean that Jesus, by his identity and his work, is uniquely suited to reconcile us to God. When I say Jesus is "unique" I mean that with the full force of the word. Nixon wasn't unique; another person under similar circumstances could have conceivably done what he did, but Jesus Christ is truly unique in his ability to bridge the gap between us as sinful people and a holy God.

Philip Melanchthon was a collaborator with Luther in the Reformation and is often thought of as its intellectual leader. He writes:

CHRIST ALONE

> When we say that we are justified by faith, we are saying nothing else than that for the sake of the Son of God we receive remission of sins and are accounted as righteous.[1]

Justified for the sake of Jesus, God's Son and for no other reason. Christ Alone.

Why Christ Alone?

Why is it that Jesus is unique in his ability to save us from our sins? Why must we trust in him alone as the only ground upon which we can be saved? The reformers emphasized Christ's unique role as Saviour in two different ways, one of which was of much greater importance 500 years ago and the other which is of greater urgency in our time. The reformers spoke of the exclusivity of Christ's identity. Jesus is unique in his ability to save because of his identity as the incarnate Son of God. Only Jesus can save. The reformers also spoke of the sufficiency of Christ's work. Jesus dying as our substitute fully atones for the sins of all who put their trust in Him. Jesus' work is enough (by itself, with nothing else before it, alongside it, under it, etc).

Exclusivity of Christ's Identity

Almost 500 years before Martin Luther posted his 95 Theses at Wittenburg, Anselm, the Archbishop of Canterbury, wrestled with the question we are asking this morning:

---

[1] Philipp Melanchthon, *The Chief Theological Topics: Loci Praecipui Theologici*, 2nd English ed., trans. J. A. O. Preus (St. Louis: Concordia, 2011), 157.

> By what logic or necessity did God become man, and by his death, as we believe and profess, restore life to the world, when he could have done this through the agency of some other, angelic or human, or simply by willing it?[2]

Why did God save us by means of Christ? Why not in some other way? Look at what the author of Hebrews says:

> For since the law has but a shadow of the good things to come instead of the true form of these realities, it can never, by the same sacrifices that are continually offered every year, make perfect those who draw near. Otherwise, would they not have ceased to be offered, since the worshipers, having once been cleansed, would no longer have any consciousness of sins? But in these sacrifices, there is a reminder of sins every year. For it is impossible for the blood of bulls and goats to take away sins (Heb. 10:1-4).

The writer to the Hebrews explains the basic answer to Anselm's question. Why didn't God save by some other means, by the blood of an animal or the sacrifice of an angel? The answer is that the blood of bulls and goats can never take away sin. The evidence he offers us is that the sacrifices were ongoing, they didn't resolve the underlying problem. The logic of this is straightforward. The price of human sin is human life. A goat cannot stand in your place before God to

---

[2] Anselm, *Why God Became Man*, in *Anselm of Canterbury: The Major Works*, ed. Brian Davies and G. R. Evans, Oxford World's Classics (Oxford: Oxford University Press, 1998), I:1.

take the penalty for your sin. Neither can an angel or anything else. The goat and the angel are not like you. They cannot represent you. The author to the Hebrews continues and explains that Jesus supersedes a sacrificial system that cannot save by becoming like the people that he is going to rescue. Look with me at verse 5: "Consequently, when Christ came into the world, he said, 'Sacrifices and offerings you have not desired, but a body have you prepared for me.'"

Jesus supersedes the system of sacrificing bulls and goats (which cannot take away sin) by taking on humanity so that he can face God's judgment as one of us, as our representative. Listen to how Paul explains this same truth in Romans:

> There is therefore now no condemnation for those who are in Christ Jesus. For the law of the Spirit of life has set you free in Christ Jesus from the law of sin and death. For God has done what the law, weakened by the flesh, could not do. By sending his own Son in the likeness of sinful flesh and for sin, he condemned sin in the flesh, in order that the righteous requirement of the law might be fulfilled in us, who walk not according to the flesh but according to the Spirit (Rom. 8:1–4).

Because of our sinful hearts we cannot keep the law and so God cannot find us to be righteous. Neither can God deal with our sin through the sacrifice of a lamb. The lamb isn't like me. Human sin demands human life. So God comes himself, but as a person, so that he can be my representative on the cross. Sin is condemned in the flesh (in the life of a person) as it must be, but not in my flesh, not in my life...in Christ's, who takes my place.

The author of Hebrews says,

> Since therefore the children share in flesh and blood, he himself likewise partook of the same things, that through death he might destroy the one who has the power of death, that is, the devil, and deliver all those who through fear of death were subject to lifelong slavery—Therefore he had to be made like his brothers in every respect, so that he might become a merciful and faithful high priest in the service of God, to make propitiation for the sins of the people (Heb. 2:14–15, 17).

Human sin requires a human life in payment. Jesus had to become like us so that he could satisfy God's judgment against sin in us. But this is only an answer to part of our question: why is salvation only found through Jesus Christ? Why couldn't I give up my life (a human life) on behalf of one of you? The simple answer to this is that I have my own debt to pay. My life is already forfeit because I have sinned and fallen short of the glory of God. But look with me again at Hebrews 10. Do you see the exchange that Jesus makes?

> Consequently, when Christ came into the world, he said, "Sacrifices and offerings you have not desired, but a body have you prepared for me; in burnt offerings and sin offerings you have taken no pleasure." Then I said, "Behold, I have come to do your will, O God, as it is written of me in the scroll of the book." When he said above, "You have neither

desired nor taken pleasure in sacrifices and offerings and burnt offerings and sin offerings" (these are offered according to the law), then he added, "Behold, I have come to do your will." He does away with the first in order to establish the second. And by that will we have been sanctified through the offering of the body of Jesus Christ once for all (Heb. 10:5-10).

A lamb cannot represent you because it isn't like you. And I cannot represent you because I have my own debt to pay. But Jesus can stand in your place because he became like you ("A body you have prepared for me") and because he lived in perfect obedience to his Father ("Behold, I have come to do your will, O God"). Jesus solves both of our problems. We have a debt to pay because of our sin and we have a life to live in obedience to God. We have done neither, but Jesus did both. I want you to see the positive aspect of this in the life of Christ:

> Then Jesus came from Galilee to the Jordan to John, to be baptized by him. John would have prevented him, saying, "I need to be baptized by you, and do you come to me?" But Jesus answered him, "Let it be so now, for thus it is fitting for us to fulfill all righteousness." Then he consented. And when Jesus was baptized, immediately he went up from the water, and behold, the heavens were opened to him, and he saw the Spirit of God descending like a dove and coming to rest on him; and behold, a voice from heaven said, "This is my beloved Son, with whom I am well pleased" (Mt. 3:13-17).

Jesus receives baptism? Why does he do this? Those who took John's baptism were expressing repentance in preparation for the arrival of the Saviour. Jesus does not need to express repentance. Jesus tells us himself in verse 15. Let this happen because it is appropriate to fulfill all righteousness. What did we read in Hebrews 10? "I have come to do your will, O God." And, as the Father looks down on the obedient Son, we hear these incredible words: "This is my beloved Son, with whom I am well pleased." Jesus didn't receive the baptism of John for his sake, but for ours. Jesus lived in obedience and earned righteousness as a human being so that righteousness could be credited to our accounts by faith.

The Sufficiency of Christ's Work
Let's return to Hebrews 10 and ponder the sufficiency of Christ's work:

> And every priest stands daily at his service, offering repeatedly the same sacrifices, which can never take away sins. But when Christ had offered for all time a single sacrifice for sins, he sat down at the right hand of God, waiting from that time until his enemies should be made a footstool for his feet. For by a single offering he has perfected for all time those who are being sanctified (Heb. 10:11–14).

The priests of old had to continually offer their sacrifices because the blood of a lamb cannot atone for sin. They were always standing; the work was never completed. But Jesus, who is uniquely suited to save us, offers himself once and then sits, having finished everything that needed to be done to rescue his people. Verse 14 is particularly important in the context of the Reformation and our interactions with Roman Catholics because it established the sufficiency of Christ's work while distinguishing between justification and sanctification.

Jesus offering of himself perfects you (justification) and begins the process of reforming you (sanctification). It perfects those who are being perfected. The father looks upon you and sees the perfection of his son in you even as you work out your salvation over a lifetime of following Christ.

Christ Alone in the Reformation

I want to pause here for a minute and talk about the impact of Christ *alone* in the time of the reformation and how it differs in our day. The Catholic church and the reformers were generally in agreement on the exclusivity of Christ's identity, at least on a theoretical level. The main point of contention was on the sufficiency of Christ's work. The reformers were deeply concerned that the sacraments and customs of the church eroded the sufficiency of Christ's work.

Thomas Aquinas was a Roman Catholic philosopher and theologian who lived a few hundred years before Luther posted his 95 theses, and his writing is helpful for understanding what the reformers were reacting to. Aquinas writes: "Christ's Passion [Jesus' sacrifice on our behalf] works its effect in them to whom it is applied, through faith and charity and the sacraments of faith."[3] Since Christ's Passion preceded as a kind of universal cause of the forgiveness of sins, it needs to be applied to each for the

---

[3] http://dhspriory.org/thomas/summa/TP/TP049.html#TPQ49O UTP1.

cleansing of personal sins. Now this is done by baptism and penance and the other sacraments, which derive their power from Christ's Passion.

Can you see why the reformers were concerned here? If regeneration is mediated through baptism and forgiveness is obtained in the confessional, if justification is deepened by communion and temporal sins are paid through the fire of purgatory, when all of these rituals and sacraments and people stand between me and the effect of Christ's work, then it cannot be said that Christ's work is sufficient. If I need all of these other things to get at the effect of Christ's work, then Christ's work is no longer sufficient by itself to save me. This is an ongoing issue in our day. The sufficiency of Christ's work is still undermined by all of these traditions and rituals and sacraments that exist in the Catholic church.

But in addition to that, the exclusive identity of Christ is under far greater threat than it was 500 years ago. The idea that salvation is found exclusively in Christ Jesus would be offensive to many in the mainstream today who are perfectly fine with other people finding their own way to God. Christ is good for me, but my friend has found their way through Islam and that's good for them. This sola, Christ alone, pushes back directly against that modern way of thinking. There are not many pathways to God; there is only Christ. Christ alone is able, because of his exclusive identity and sufficient work, to rescue sinners and reconcile them to a holy God.

Exhortation

I would like to draw this chapter to a close with a few thoughts in application for us. Earlier, we referred to Jesus' baptism. Jesus received John's baptism of repentance, not for himself, but as our representative, to fulfill all righteousness. I want you to take this single example and blow it up in your mind into every corner of your life. I want you to think of everything that you should be and do because God made you for his glory. As a father or a mother, as a son or a daughter, as a brother or a sister, as a man or women, young or old…in so many ways we have transgressed by sinning against God and by being negligent to bring him glory as he designed us to do. I want you to think of a specific sin, a specific way that you have failed to be what God made you to be. The blood of Jesus Christ atones for that specific sin and the righteousness of Jesus Christ fills up that failure.

In Christ, your guilt and debt for that sin is removed. But, more than that, the Father looks upon you as if you have thought it or felt it or done it to his glory as he intended you to. Jesus earns that lived righteousness for you and credits it to your account as though you were the one in the water with John, fulfilling all righteousness. Only Jesus possesses this, what you need to stand before God forgiven. And Jesus possesses it perfectly and completely so that you can know that you lack for nothing. How are we to respond to these things?

The author of Hebrews helps us here again:

> Therefore, brothers, since we have confidence to enter the holy places by the blood of Jesus, by the new and living way that he opened for us through the curtain, that is, through his flesh, and since we have a great priest over the house of God, let us draw near with a true heart in full assurance of faith, with our hearts sprinkled clean from an evil conscience and our bodies washed with pure water. Let us hold fast

the confession of our hope without wavering, for he who promised is faithful (Heb.10:19-23).

When you put your head on your pillow to sleep tonight and when you wake up tomorrow morning, whether you are at work or school or home, whether you are young or old, when you are victorious in fleeing from temptation and when you fail and choose to sin; in this midst of all of those things you should be absolutely confident that God loves you and is for you because of the exclusive identity and sufficient work of his Son and your Saviour, Jesus Christ.

In the words of Charles Spurgeon,

> Remember, sinner, it is not your hold of Christ that saves you. It is Christ; It is not your joy in Christ that saves you, it is Christ; It is not even faith in Christ, though that is the instrument, it is Christ's blood and merits; therefore, look not to you hope, but to Christ, the source of you hope; look not to your faith, but to Christ, the author and finisher of your faith; and if you do that, ten thousand devils cannot throw you down.[4]

It is not communion or baptism that saves us, though these are important channels for God's blessing in our lives. Jesus Christ is the exclusive and sufficient ground for your salvation. We are saved through *Christ alone*.

---

[4] Iain Murray, *The Forgotten Spurgeon* (Edinburgh: Banner of Truth, 2004), 42.

4

Faith Alone

Josh Anderson

When discussing the five solas of the Reformation, "faith alone" can sometimes come first on the list. But it is helpful for us to first understand the other solas before we tackle this one. The argument for faith in Christ as the sole means of accessing salvation is much stronger and more obvious when we have a clear understanding of faith's object, namely Jesus, as well as our own condition. Let me briefly remind you of what we've learned so far:

All human beings inherit the nature of our first father Adam and are born as sinners. In that condition we owe God a debt in payment for our sin as well as a life perfectly lived. We can do neither of those things ourselves, and God will not allow sin to go unpunished.

Jesus is uniquely suited to save because he fills both of our deficiencies. He takes on humanity and lives as the second Adam, except he accomplishes everything perfectly and entirely without sin. Jesus, as the son of God, is perfectly righteous in himself, but through the incarnation He earns righteousness as one of us, as our representative. Then he gives up his own life to take our place in the pathway of God's wrath. He pays our debt for sin. Then he mediates between the Father and us, hiding us in himself so that, when the Father looks at us, he sees us through the goodness of the Son that He loves. Judgement removed, righteousness obtained, reconciliation achieved—not by me, but by Christ. And not by anyone else. Not by Mary, not by a pope, not by a local priest, not because of baptism or purgatory. Only through Christ can you obtain what you need to be reconciled to God.

Given all of that—my inability to solve this life-threatening problem and Christ's perfect, complete solution—it seems inevitable to me that casting myself at the feet of Jesus and putting all of my hope on him is the only possible answer to my dilemma. How else could I solve my problem except by faith? And, yet, this did not seem necessary or sufficient to many in Luther's day, and it doesn't seem necessary or sufficient to many in our day.

I would like to do two things in this chapter. I'd like to show you, from the Word of God, that faith in Christ and nothing else is the only way that you can be justified before God. It is the only way that God can look at you and say, I am well pleased with this one, my child. Faith and faith alone is the only way that we can be saved. And then I'd like us to explore the relationship between faith and works, particularly in light of James 2:24, "You see that a person is justified by works and not by faith alone."

Biblical Evidence
The Scriptural argument for the necessity of faith goes deep. By that, I mean that the argument for the necessity of faith is rigorously developed and explained by the inspired writers.

Between the books of Romans and Galatians (two books which have this subject in view), there are dozens of references to justification or salvation coming through faith and full explanations for why this is the case.

But the argument for salvation through faith is also wide. By that, I mean that it is woven throughout Scripture. It shows up all over the place even when it isn't the particular subject in view. A small sampling of verses that teach us that we are saved by believing could include:

> For God so loved the world, that he gave his only Son, that whoever believes in him should not perish but have eternal life (John 3:16);

> Therefore, since we have been justified by faith, we have peace with God through our Lord Jesus Christ. Through him we have also obtained access by faith into this grace in which we stand, and we rejoice in hope of the glory of God (Rom. 5:1-2);

> ...my speech and my message were not in plausible words of wisdom, but in demonstration of the Spirit and of power, 5 that your faith might not rest in the wisdom of men but in the power of God (1 Cor. 2:4-5);

> For by grace you have been saved through faith. And this is not your own doing; it is the gift of God, 9 not a result of works, so that no one may boast (Eph. 2:8);

> [that I may] be found in him, not having a righteousness of my own that comes from the law,

> but that which comes through faith in Christ, the righteousness from God that depends on faith (Phil. 3:9).

Romans, Corinthians, Galatians, Ephesians, Philippians...do you see? We could go on, but for the sake of time I will just say that the Scriptural evidence for the necessity of faith is overwhelming. But this is not enough, because we are not only saying that faith is necessary but that faith *and nothing else* is the way that we are justified before God. Not faith and then a life well lived. Not faith and then regular confession. Not faith and then faithful giving. Not faith and then prayer to saints. We may do at least some of these things as part of our Christian walk, but they do not contribute to the righteousness that we need to be saved. Paul explains why faith stands alone in securing righteousness for us in Galatians 5.

> For freedom Christ has set us free; stand firm therefore, and do not submit again to a yoke of slavery. Look: I, Paul, say to you that if you accept circumcision, Christ will be of no advantage to you. I testify again to every man who accepts circumcision that he is obligated to keep the whole law. You are severed from Christ, you who would be justified by the law; you have fallen away from grace. For through the Spirit, by faith, we ourselves eagerly wait for the hope of righteousness. For in Christ Jesus neither circumcision nor uncircumcision counts for anything, but only faith working through love (Gal. 5:1–5).

From verses 2-4, Paul makes two parallel statements with an explanation sandwiched in between. I'm going to make it a bit easier for you to see Paul's argument in the text:

v2 if you accept circumcision
Christ will be of no advantage to you

v3 I testify again to every man who accepts circumcision that he is obligated to keep the whole law

v4 you who would be justified by the law
You are severed from Christ

Accepting circumcision and attempting to be justified by the law are the same idea. They are lined up on the left. What Paul means in today's language is the attempt to work to earn God's favor. Or, to turn that around, to see my own goodness as all or part of the reason that God has saved me and loves me.

Paul warns the Galatians and us that if we lean, even in part, upon our own goodness, then we are severed from Christ and he is of no advantage to us. The righteousness that Christ earned, his exclusive identity and sufficient work- these are no longer of any benefit to me if I seek justification through law-keeping. Why is that? Why can't it be that I trust in Jesus but then also add to my justification by doing good works, by keeping God's laws? Why can't it be that God accepts me as good first because I've trusted in Jesus' work but then, increasingly, because I am actually good?

Paul's explanation is sandwiched in verse 3: "every man who accepts circumcision is obligated to keep the whole law." The law is an all-or-nothing prospect. There is no credit for partial completion. It's a pass or fail kind of test. There is no middle ground with God's law. Either we do it all and we are law-keepers, or we break any part of it and become law-breakers.

One way of understanding of this is not in terms of earning righteousness by works, but in terms of how sin pollutes our souls. If I take a pail of pure, clean water and put the smallest drop of e-coli into that bucket, could we go to any part of the bucket and say, "this part is pure water?" Of course not! Even it it's only 1 parts per billion or 1 part per trillion, the whole pail is contaminated. If I am going to lean, in any way, upon my own righteousness for acceptance before God, then my righteousness must be pure. I'd need to keep every single part of God's law in every part of my life. In thought, word, and deed. Sleeping or awake. From infancy until my final moments on this earth. There can be absolutely zero parts per million or billion of sin in me or my righteousness is contaminated. If we make law keeping the foundation of even part of our standing before God, Paul warns us that we have been cut off from Christ.

Another way of conceiving of this is to imagine a fork in the road. One signpost reads, "law-keeping" and the other sign reads "faith in Christ". There is no central pathway. There is no road that reads, "99% Christ, 1% law keeping". You can have all of Jesus' righteousness: a human life, lived perfectly to the glory of the Father, and payment for your sin through his substitutionary death on the cross. You can have all of that, or you can have your own righteousness. But we cannot form a mixed foundation upon which to stand before God. Dependence on our own infected righteousness (in any amount) invalidates the whole thing. Paul speaks of the Israelites' failure to grasp this in Romans 9:

What shall we say, then? That Gentiles who did not pursue righteousness have attained it, that is, a righteousness that is by faith; but that Israel who pursued a law that would lead to righteousness did not succeed in reaching that law. Why? Because they did not pursue it by faith, but as if it were based on works. They have stumbled over the stumbling stone, as it is written, "Behold, I am laying in Zion a stone of stumbling, and a rock of offense; and whoever believes in him will not be put to shame" (Rom. 9:30-33).

Paul doesn't say that it was a mistake to pursue the law. The mistake was to think that righteousness could be obtained through that pursuit. They pursued the law as if God intended them to obtain righteousness through it, but that was never the idea. Righteousness has always been obtained through faith.

Faith and Works
If I were having this conversation with the priest at the Catholic church around the corner from our home, I expect that he would object, "What about James 2:24! This is the only place in the Bible where your exact phrase is used, and James says that we are not justified by faith alone." This is a fair question, and it gets to the heart of the confusion. Let's look at two different passages that speak about the relationship between faith and works: Romans 4:1-5 and James 2:14-26.

What then shall we say was gained by Abraham, our forefather according to the flesh? For if Abraham was

> justified by works, he has something to boast about, but not before God. For what does the Scripture say? "Abraham believed God, and it was counted to him as righteousness." Now to the one who works, his wages are not counted as a gift but as his due. And to the one who does not work but believes in him who justifies the ungodly, his faith is counted as righteousness... (Rom. 4:1-5).

What did Abraham obtain? Righteousness. How did he obtain it? By faith. Abraham believed God, and righteousness was credited to him. Abraham does not earn the righteousness as a wage the way we earn money for our labour. He obtains it as a gift through faith. Paul's purpose is to help us understand how we receive righteousness. The answer is: by faith.

Now, I'm going to provide a longer section of James so we can get the full sense of his argument:

> What good is it, my brothers, if someone says he has faith but does not have works? Can that faith save him? If a brother or sister is poorly clothed and lacking in daily food, and one of you says to them, "Go in peace, be warmed and filled," without giving them the things needed for the body, what good is that? So also faith by itself, if it does not have works, is dead. But someone will say, 'You have faith and I have works.' Show me your faith apart from your works, and I will show you my faith by my works. You believe that God is one; you do well. Even the demons believe—and shudder! Do you want to be shown, you foolish person, that faith apart from works is useless? Was not Abraham our father

justified by works when he offered up his son Isaac on the altar? You see that faith was active along with his works, and faith was completed by his works; and the Scripture was fulfilled that says, "Abraham believed God, and it was counted to him as righteousness"—and he was called a friend of God. You see that a person is justified by works and not by faith alone. And in the same way was not also Rahab the prostitute justified by works when she received the messengers and sent them out by another way? For as the body apart from the spirit is dead, so also faith apart from works is dead (Ja. 2:14-26).

What is James trying to teach us here? James' goal is different than Paul's in Romans 4. Paul is explaining how we receive righteousness, but James is teaching us about the nature of faith; saving faith always produces the fruit of good works. We don't have enough time to work through it meticulously, but I think verses 18-19 illustrate the question that James is trying to answer:

But someone will say, "You have faith and I have works." Show me your faith apart from your works, and I will show you my faith by my works. You believe that God is one; you do well. Even the demons believe—and shudder!

James is concerned about people who would say that it is possible to believe in Jesus and remain unchanged. In response to this, James warns them that not all belief is saving faith. The demons believe but they are not saved, they are not transformed. There is no evidence because their faith is a dead faith. We sometimes compare the process of regeneration to the transformation of a caterpillar into a butterfly. The caterpillar goes into the cocoon and emerges as a new creature, a butterfly. Have you ever seen a butterfly scrunched up on a tree branch, crawling along? Of course not! Butterflies fly, they don't crawl. It's not in their nature to act that way anymore. It's in their new nature to fly, and so they do. Their flight doesn't transform them; it demonstrates the change that has already occurred.

Rather than caterpillars and butterflies, James provides them with an illustration of the life of Abraham. What is interesting here is that Paul (in Romans 4) and James both quote from the same portion from Genesis:

> And he brought him outside and said, "Look toward heaven, and number the stars, if you are able to number them." Then he said to him, "So shall your offspring be." And he believed the LORD, and he counted it to him as righteousness (Gen. 15:5-6).

But, James' illustration actually comes from Genesis 22, many years later, when Abraham takes the promised son Isaac up on the mountain to sacrifice him to God. James points to Abraham's obedience on the mountain and tells us that this is the fulfillment of the Scriptures in Genesis 15. Are we to understand that Abraham wasn't justified until he took Isaac up on the mountain almost 30 years after God declares that his faith was counted to him as righteousness? Or could it be that James is telling us that Abraham's obedience was the evidence that his faith was real and living, effective and God-granted?

In the simplest terms, the Catholic church's position is that faith is necessary but insufficient. This from the council of Trent, the Catholic response to the Reformation:

> Having, therefore, been thus justified, and made the friends and domestics of God, advancing from virtue to virtue, they are renewed, as the Apostle says, day by day; that is, by mortifying the members of their own flesh, and by presenting them as instruments of justice unto sanctification, they, through the observance of the commandments of God and of the Church, faith co-operating with good works, increase in that justice which they have received through the grace of Christ, and are still further justified.[1]

That may be a little difficult to follow. The key part for us this morning is the end. "Faith co-operating with good works, increase in that justice which they have received through the grace of Christ, and are still further justified." So I am contributing to my justification. By my good works, I am further justified today than I was yesterday when I believed in Christ. But that isn't what the Bible teaches. "To the one who does not work but believes in him who justifies the ungodly, his faith is counted as righteousness." (Rom. 4:5) Our works are the fruit of our justification, not its cause or foundation. The importance of this cannot be overstated.

If you stand on a mixed foundation of Christ's work and your work, then you lose the benefits of Christ's righteousness. This means that you must stand on your own merit before God. The difference between these two options

---

[1] http://www.thecounciloftrent.com/ch6.htm.

is vast and massive for your life. It's the difference between waking up tomorrow morning in a cold sweat because you are behind on your righteousness, and waking up with the knowledge that God is for you and loves you despite the hard truth that you will sin again today. There is a precious freedom in knowing that God's love for you does not ebb and flow in response to your failures and victories in the Christian life, because your righteousness is not obtained through that obedience but through faith in the perfect Son of God.

Salvation is only found in Christ because only Christ has what we need to be reconciled to God. We stand entirely on the foundation of Christ's exclusive identity and sufficient work through faith. Don't mix these foundations! Put your full weight on Christ by faith, and know that God loves you unshakably for the sake of his Son.

5

GRACE ALONE

Alexander Kloosterman

"We are beggars. This is true." Martin Luther[1]

These were the final written words of a man who had not only spent decades expounding the truth that we are saved by grace *alone,* but who had also been profoundly shaped by such truth. He realized, even in spite of his enormous accomplishments, that his only hope before God was not in his *bringing,* but in his *begging.* Timothy George, commenting on these famous last words, wrote:

> Luther's whole approach to the Christian life is summed up in these last words. The posture of the human vis a vis God is one of utter receptivity. We have no legs of our own on which to stand. No mystical "ground of the soul" can serve as a basis of our union with the divine. We can earn no merits

---

[1] Timothy George, *Theology of the Reformers, Revised Edition* (Nashville, TN: B&H Academic, 2013), 105.

that will purchase for us a standing before God. We are beggars—needy, vulnerable, totally bereft of resources with which to save ourselves. For Luther, the good news of the gospel was that in Jesus Christ God had become a beggar too. God identified with us in our neediness. Like the good Samaritan who exposed himself to the dangers of the road to attend to the dying man in the ditch, God "came where we were."[2]

The reformation was, among other things, a recovery of the precious truth that we are saved by grace alone: "For by grace you have been saved through faith. And this is not your own doing; it is the gift of God, not a result of works, so that no one may boast" (Eph. 2:8-9). The Scriptures testify that salvation is fundamentally a gift to be received by faith, not the reward for our works. We didn't earn it. We don't deserve it. We didn't achieve it. We can't step back in any way and say, "that was me."

However, beyond celebrating the recovery of the gospel *back then*, I want us to see the ongoing need to recover the gospel *now*. This battle for the recovery of salvation by grace alone was *not* a new battle; nor was it the last time the church of Jesus Christ would have to refute false understandings of salvation by grace, and clarify the truth of the gospel. This struggle continues even today, and the reason why it continues is that the human heart, apart from Christ, has always been and always will be opposed to the grace of God. The human heart loves to *boast*. We say, "I'm really not that bad," "the problem is them not me," "I'm a good person,"

---

[2] Timothy George, *Theology of the Reformers*, 105.

"I'm better than most people," or "I can make up for my wrongs." This resistance to God's grace is not a uniquely catholic problem. It is not a uniquely medieval problem. It is a *human* problem. Why? Because we are proud, and grace humbles us. Grace disarms us of the illusion of total control. It robs us of our boasting and dismantles our trust in our goodness and self-righteousness. It confronts us with our total spiritual inability, and the devastating effects of sin. Grace reminds us of our helplessness and desperate *need* for saving—that we cannot be our own savior. Since grace is the enemy of human pride and self-exaltation, we have resisted and opposed God's grace since the fall.

In this brief chapter, I want to begin to answer the question, "Why must the doctrine of *sola gratia* continue to be carefully articulated and defended today?" To do so I will first attempt to demonstrate that self-exaltation is opposed to God's grace, and that self-exaltation is a problem of all sinful humanity. Second, I will briefly consider how this problem has been manifested throughout history, and is indeed the "spirit of our age "(1 Cor. 2:6-6). Lastly, I will consider from Scripture the true condition of humanity, and the good news that salvation is by grace alone by examining our *need* for salvation, the *cause* of our salvation, God's gracious *work* in saving us, and God's ultimate *goal* of our salvation.

Grace and Self-Exaltation
In the Bible, God's work of salvation by grace alone is repeatedly contrasted with human boasting and self-exaltation. Paul writes: "For by grace you have been saved through faith. And this is not your own doing; it is the gift of God, not a result of works, so that no one may boast" (Eph. 2:8-9).

One of God's purposes in salvation by grace alone is the silencing of human self-exaltation. God accomplishes this by removing all ground for boasting (1 Cor. 1:29; Judges 7:2). The essence of human boasting is this: attributing to self what should only be attributed to God. Why did God reduce Gideon's army from over 30 000 to 300? We are told it was to silence their boasting:

> The Lord said to Gideon, "The people with you are too many for me to give the Midianites into their hand, lest Israel boast over me, saying, 'My own hand has saved me'" (Judges 7:2).

Human boasting is antithetical to salvation by grace alone, and is rooted in the self-exalting nature of sinful mankind. A helpful passage of Scripture that exposes the antithesis between boastful self-exaltation and grace is found in the Gospel of Luke:

> He also told this parable to some who trusted in themselves that they were righteous, and treated others with contempt: "Two men went up into the temple to pray, one a Pharisee and the other a tax collector. The Pharisee, standing by himself, prayed thus: 'God, I thank you that I am not like other men, extortioners, unjust, adulterers, or even like this tax collector. I fast twice a week; I give tithes of all that I get.' But the tax collector, standing far off, would not even lift up his eyes to heaven, but beat his breast, saying, 'God, be merciful to me, a sinner!'" I tell you, this man went down to his house justified, rather than the other. For everyone who exalts

himself will be humbled, but the one who humbles himself will be exalted (Luke 18:9–14).

First, we see from the end of the parable that the two men represent two postures towards God. The Pharisee represents those who exalt themselves. This self-exaltation will ultimately result in being humbled by God, and not justified before him. The tax collector, on the other hand, demonstrated humility as he threw himself wholeheartedly upon the mercy of God. Rather than trust in himself, he despaired of himself. He was aware of both his miserable and hopeless condition before God, and the mercy of God. In other words, he was fully dependent upon the grace of God alone. The Pharisee was marked by self-righteousness and self-confidence. He boasted of his own works (fasting and tithing), even as he offered a pretentious prayer. Significantly, this prayer illustrates the human proclivity to attempt to mix grace and works. Though he seems to acknowledge that God played some role in his life, the Pharisee does indeed thank *God* for how good he is. He was not trusting in God's mercy *alone*, but in himself and his own righteousness.

The controversy surrounding the reformation did not arise because there was no previous concept of grace. Rather, the battle was over whether or not salvation is by grace *alone*. According to Scripture, there is no other kind of salvation:

> But if it is by grace, it is no longer on the basis of works; otherwise grace would no longer be grace (Rom. 11:6).

To attempt to mix our works with God's grace, as the Pharisee did, is to distort both. In order to maintain his sense of self-righteousness, the Pharisee actually had to distort God's standard, and falsely elevate himself as meeting that standard. He focused on outward works (fasting, tithing) that he could accomplish and, in so doing, implied that he did not sin in the ways others did. But Jesus taught that the problem of sin runs much deeper:

> But I say to you that everyone who looks at a woman with lustful intent has already committed adultery with her in his heart (Matt. 5:28);

> For out of the heart come evil thoughts, murder, adultery, sexual immorality, theft, false witness, slander. These are what defile a person (Matt. 15:19-20).

Self-exaltation can only flourish amidst self-deception. By deceiving himself about the nature of sin, the Pharisee was able to convince himself he wasn't really that bad. He didn't see himself as a sinner, but a righteous person. He thought he was better than others, and looked down on them. God was not his Savior but, at best, his helper.

This parable contrasts the difference between the Christian gospel and all the man-made religions of the world. Man-made religions are all an attempt of mankind to exalt himself, to say, "I am good. I am better than others. I am righteous. I do not need forgiveness. I am sovereign. I am in control." The gospel is not a call to striving, achieving, or earning. It is the end of boasting in self, and instead a call to receive Christ, by grace, through faith:

> But God chose what is foolish in the world to shame the wise; God chose what is weak in the world to shame the strong; God chose what is low and despised in the world, even things that are not, to bring to nothing things that are, so that no human being might boast in the presence of God. And because of him you are in Christ Jesus, who became to us wisdom from God, righteousness and sanctification and redemption, so that, as it is written, "Let the one who boasts, boast in the Lord" (1 Cor. 1:27-31).

Self-Exaltation A Human Problem

This human pride and self-exaltation was not confined to one individual, in one place, at one time. It is a characteristic of all fallen, sinful mankind, and has continued to be manifested through history in different ways at different times. In the fourth and fifth centuries, the early church battled the false teaching of a British monk named Pelagius, who took issue with Augustine's theology of grace. At the heart of his teaching was a denial of original sin, an emphasis on human autonomy, and the ability to achieve salvation through one's own effort and moral improvement.[3] In essence, it was "we may have gotten ourselves into this problem, it's not that bad, and we can certainly get ourselves out of it." Indeed, although his teaching was formally condemned as heresy, the heart of it remained because its substance remained in the hearts of mankind.

---

[3] Michael Horton. "Sola Gratia". In *After Darkness, Light,* Ed. R.C. Sproul Jr. (Phillipsburg, NJ: P&R Publishing, 2003), 112.

This was evident especially at the time of the Reformation. According to Michael Horton, the Reformers "recognized that pelagianism was the working theology of their day, although it remained officially condemned."[4] We must not overlook the significance of this statement. Despite the fact that pelagianism had been formally condemned as heresy, it was not only present, but widespread. This is because human beings are functional pelagians. We are not born reformed. In our sinful condition, we underestimate our problem and overestimate our abilities. In other words, we have the problem of pride and self-exaltation. Pelagianism is simply a manifestation of our human pride, and is thus reoccurring.

Our Present Ministry Context: "New Pelagianism"
Despite the fact that many do not employ this term anymore, this view is the dominant view of our own day. Michael Horton goes so far as to describe modernity as "a secularized pelagianism." He describes this "new pelagianism" in these words:

> the human being is no longer regarded as in every way dependent upon, or even answerable to, a Creator, but is treated as a self-sufficient creator in his or her own right, constructing reality in whatever shape autonomous reason, volition, and emotion determine. Sin, instead of being viewed as an offense against a holy God, is seen merely as wrongs committed against other people, or simply as offenses against oneself. This requires a program for

---

[4] *After Darkness, Light*, 112.

individual and social transformation, not the announcement of divine rescue.[5]

William Ernest Henley wrote in 1875, the poem *Invictus*. This poem has been used as inspiration my many, including Nelson Mandella during his long times of imprisonment. It helpfully captures the spirit of the age:

> Out of the night that covers me,
>   Black as the pit from pole to pole,
> I thank whatever gods may be
>   For my unconquerable soul.
>
> In the fell clutch of circumstance
> I have not winced nor cried aloud.
> Under the bludgeonings of chance
> My head is bloody, but unbowed.
>
> Beyond this place of wrath and tears
>   Looms but the Horror of the shade,
> And yet the menace of the years
>   Finds and shall find me unafraid.
>
> It matters not how strait the gate,
> How charged with punishments the scroll,
>   I am the master of my fate,
>   I am the captain of my soul.[6]

---

[5] *After Darkness, Light,* 113–114.
[6] William Ernest Henley, *Invictus.*

"I am the master of my fate, I am the captain of my soul." In this view, we are sovereign. We are above judgement. We are unconquerable. We don't need saving. We are proud. "God helps those who help themselves" has turned into "Whatever help I need will come from me."

Charles Taylor helpfully describes the secular age in which we live as the "age of authenticity."[7] In summary, this view says that to be authentic is to be true to oneself, and free from external constraints or pressures to conform. The individual is the locus of reality and truth. The highest moral value, necessarily, is the right for absolute *choice*.

Of course, one major problem with identifying the individual as the final authority to determine truth is that it is not *actually* possible for *all* individuals to adopt this view. This "expressive individualism" is an empty charade. The individual is not actually protected and upheld, but rather, destroyed. It is impossible for every individual to express themselves in ways that do not simultaneously limit the ability of other individuals to express themselves. We are seeing the chaos of such a worldview in our political and ethical discussions, particularly surrounding human sexuality and abortion.

Since the individual's rights must be protected at all costs, and yet, we cannot actually protect competing "rights" in the same way, there will always need to be a decision regarding whose "rights" to protect. This must necessarily be done with power through coercion.

---

[7] For an accessible summary of Taylor's thought and insight, see James K.A. Smith, *How (Not) To Be Secular: Reading Charles Taylor* (Grand Rapids, MI: Eerdmans, 2014).

A prime example of this incoherence is the abortion debate. It is hardly debated anymore whether or not the unborn baby is a human individual; and yet, the loud chant of those in favour of this horror is "Choice!" The moral weight of this word surpasses any argument or evidence. The ultimate evil is not to *do* evil, but to limit an individual's choice or ability to determine what evil is. Of course, this presents a clear example of the incoherence of such a worldview. Why are the 'choices' of the weak individual not protected in the same degree as those of the strong? Because this isn't really about *everyone's* choice, but *my* choice. The weak and vulnerable individuals will always suffer under this worldview. Regarding issues of sexuality, the moral decision is the one that allows for ultimate self-expression. We seem to be reaching a climax of chaos as this worldview is pushed to its limits in the practises surrounding the transgender movement.

Aside from being incoherent and dangerous, this worldview is predicated upon a distorted view of mankind. In an attempt to exalt ourselves, we have actually *lost* a realistic understanding of ourselves. This, in relation to the topic at hand, has blinded us to our need for grace. We might say that we live in an age that glories in our self-exaltation. It is into this world that the gospel shines as a light, exposing our great need and the amazing grace God has given to meet that need.

The Need for Knowledge of Self and God
The "spirit of the age," however, is antithetical to the gospel of Jesus Christ. We cannot begin to grasp the grace of God if we do not have an accurate understanding of ourselves and our own profound *need*. Self-exaltation can only flourish with self-deception. Self-exaltation is not the response to our true

selves and condition, but an illusion that we deceitfully maintain. John Calvin noted the need for an accurate view of self and God in the opening of his *Institutes:*

> Our wisdom, if it is to be thought genuine, consists almost entirely of two parts: the knowledge of God and of ourselves. As these are closely connected, it is not easy to decide which comes first and gives rise to the other. To begin with, no one can assess himself without turning his thoughts towards the God in whom he lives and moves...[8]

This knowledge causes us to despair of ourselves and see our need for God:

> So our feelings of ignorance, vanity, need, weakness and general depravity remind us that in the Lord, and no one else, can be found the true light of light of wisdom...Our evil ways make us think of all the good things of God. We can never really seek him in earnest until we begin to despair of ourselves. Don't we all rely on our own strength when we are not aware of our real nature and are quite content with our own gifts, ignoring our misery? When we do come to ourselves, we are spurred on to seek God and are led by his hand to find him.[9]

---

[8] John Calvin. *Institutes of the Christian Religion,* Ed. Tony Lane and Hilary Osborne (Grand Rapids, MI: Baker Academic, 1987), 21.
[9] Calvin, *Institutes of the Christian Religion,* 22.

However, this knowledge of ourselves cannot come by looking at ourselves, but rather, to God. Calvin writes:

> On the other hand, it is evident that man never arrives at true self-knowledge before he has looked into the face of God and then comes away to look at himself. For (such is our innate pride) we always seem to ourselves just and upright, wise and holy until we are convinced, by clear proof, of our injustice and deviousness, stupidity and impurity. However, we are never convinced of this if we simply look to ourselves and not to the Lord as well, since he is the only yardstick from which this conviction can come. For since we all have the tendency to hypocrisy, any hollow appearance of righteousness is quite enough to satisfy us instead of righteousness itself…It is like an eye which has never been shown anything other than black, assessing an object which is really off-white or discoloured as pure white.[10]

But where will be find such knowledge of God and ourselves? As Calvin affirms, it is only by the Spirit working through the word that we come to such knowledge of God and ourselves:

> And we all, with unveiled face, beholding the glory of the Lord, are being transformed into the same image from one degree of glory to another. For this comes from the Lord who is the Spirit (2 Cor. 3:18);

---

[10] Calvin, *Institutes of the Christian Religion*, 22.

> For God, who said, "Let light shine out of darkness," has shone in our hearts to give the light of the knowledge of the glory of God in the face of Jesus Christ" (2 Cor. 4:6).

It is no coincidence that a biblical understanding of salvation by grace alone was recovered at the same time that the written word of God was being read and restored to the people of God. We cannot understand God's grace if we do not understand our state of misery. Indeed, all illusions of self-righteousness and ability come crashing down before the word of God. The only sure place to look in order to understand ourselves and our condition, as well as the grace God has provided, is not our experience, but Scripture. There are few passages of Scripture that give such a vivid description of our salvation by grace alone than those written in the letter of Paul to the Ephesian church:

> And you were dead in the trespasses and sins in which you once walked, following the course of this world, following the prince of the power of the air, the spirit that is now at work in the sons of disobedience— among whom we all once lived in the passions of our flesh, carrying out the desires of the body and the mind, and were by nature children of wrath, like the rest of mankind. But God, being rich in mercy, because of the great love with which he loved us, even when we were dead in our trespasses, made us alive together with Christ—by grace you have been saved— and raised us up with him and seated us with him in the heavenly places in Christ Jesus, so that in the coming ages he might show the

immeasurable riches of his grace in kindness toward us in Christ Jesus. For by grace you have been saved through faith. And this is not your own doing; it is the gift of God, not a result of works, so that no one may boast. For we are his workmanship, created in Christ Jesus for good works, which God prepared beforehand, that we should walk in them (Eph. 2:1-10).

Reading Ephesians 2:1-10 is like sitting in a doctor's office and hearing the worst diagnosis you could ever imagine, but then having the joy of being informed that there is a perfect, indestructible cure. Through this passage, God reveals the devastating effects of sin and our powerless state to change things. We are *totally* lost and unable to do anything about it. And yet, there is a cure for our state that cannot fail: *salvation by Grace alone, through faith alone, in Christ alone.* From this passage (Ephesians 2:110), we must understand four things about this glorious salvation: 1) our desperate *need* for salvation, 2) the *cause* of our salvation being the love of God, 3) the gracious *work* of God in our salvation, and 4) the *goal* of God saving us by grace.

The need for saving by grace alone:
Dead, enslaved, condemned (vv. 1-3)
We cannot understand the riches of God's grace if we do not understand our problem. A life vest is only good news for those who are drowning, not those safely at shore. Unless we understand the depth of our sin and its consequences, grace will appear unnecessary, like the antidote to a disease we do not truly believe we have.

In this passage, Paul contrasts life before we were in Christ with life after we are in Christ. Before Christ, we see three dreadful realities: we are dead, enslaved, condemned—and helpless to do anything about it. In other words, we were in desperate *need* of saving.

The first description Paul gives of life outside of Christ is devastating: We all were dead:
"And you were dead in the trespasses and sins in which you once walked" (v. 1). As noted, Paul is not only referring to his audience, but to "all of mankind" as he will later state in verse 3. The consequences of the fall are not confined to some people, but affect all people. One commentator writes:

> The spiritual state of the readers when they were outside of Christ, as well as of the rest of humanity, is death. The apostle's description is not that of some particularly decadent tribe or degraded segment of society, or even of the extremely corrupt paganism of his own day. Rather, it is the biblical diagnosis of fallen man in fallen society everywhere.[11]

We are either "in Christ," or "in trespasses and sins." This truth should humble us, and is a death-blow to self-exaltation. Remember, contempt for others and comparing our works to theirs is a deceitful means we employ to convince ourselves we are in no real need. But here, Paul makes explicit that all mankind suffers from the same condition: death. As Aleksandr Solzhenitsyn wrote in *The Gulag Archipelago:*

---

[11] Peter Thomas O'Brien, *The Letter to the Ephesians*, PNTC (Grand Rapids, MI: W.B. Eerdmans Publishing Co., 1999), 156.

> If only it were all so simple! If only there were evil people somewhere insidiously committing evil deeds, and it were necessary only to separate them from the rest of us and destroy them. But the line dividing good and evil cuts through the heart of every human being. And who is willing to destroy a piece of his own heart?[12]

The consequence of sin is death—spiritual, and finally, physical. As Paul says elsewhere, "the wages of sin is death" (Rom. 6:23). The spiritual death Paul describes in this passage refers to a state of alienation from the life of God (Eph. 4:18). In other words, death is personal and relational. Paul describes this spiritual death in his letter to the Romans:

> as it is written: "None is righteous, no, not one; no one understands; no one seeks for God. All have turned aside; together they have become worthless; no one does good, not even one" (Rom 3:10-12).

We don't know God, and we don't want to. We don't love him. We don't need him. This death has left us alienated from Christ, without any hope of changing our condition (2:12). In death, we are utterly helpless. What a dead person needs is resurrection, not a helping hand—and a dead person cannot raise themselves. A dead person does not contribute to their resurrection. A biblical understanding of our spiritual condition apart from Christ removes any foundation of works that we might hope to contribute to our salvation. If anything

---

[12] Aleksandr I. Solzhenitsyn. *The Gulag Archipelago Abridged,* (New York, NY: HarperCollins, 2007).

can be done, it won't be done by us. It will need to be the work of God, by grace alone.

The second description Paul gives of our condition apart from Christ is that of being enslaved. Peter O'Brien writes, "The reader's former lifestyle, which characterizes all who are outside of Christ, was not true freedom but evidence of a fearful bondage to forces over which they had no control."[13] This is a reality-check for our culture that views humans as free, autonomous beings. It confronts us with the reality that our choices are *not* neutral, but heavily influenced by outside forces. We are slaves, and we don't even know it.

Ephesians 2:2-3 shows that, before Christ, we were under the powerful influence of three forces: i) the world, ii) the flesh, and iii) the devil.

i) We were in bondage to the "course of this world." The worldly ways are not merely the latest trends in fashion, but rather, "society's attitudes, habits, and preferences, which were alien to God and his standards."[14] We like to think we are willing to stand against the crowd, but Scripture tells us we simply go along with the course of this world. The popular cultural archetype of the "hero" is a powerful image, but it is not us. We are the crowd.

ii) We "lived in the passions of our flesh," which is our whole sinful being. The fact that we "carried out the desires of the body and the mind" reveals that we did *what we wanted to do*. We are not enslaved because we can't gain the freedom we desire; we are enslaved in that we desire what enslaves. *We* are the problem. We need freedom from *us*. Again, this

---

[13] O'Brien, *The Letter to the Ephesians*, 156.
[14] O'Brien, *The Letter to the Ephesians*, 159.

condition of bondage reveals our great need, and total inability.

iii) Lastly, we were under the influence of powerful, personal forces, "following the prince of the power of the air, the spirit that is now at work in the sons of disobedience." This is our enemy, the devil.

The third and final description Paul gives of our condition is that we were *condemned*. He writes that we were "by nature children of wrath." This reveals that sin is not merely something we *do*. It is a result of *who we are*. We sin because we are sinners. And the consequence for who we are and what we do is the wrath of a personal God.

This is one of the more offensive truths of the gospel: that we are condemned. One way we seek to get around our sense of guilt is by attempting to separate who we are from what we do. I was watching a show, and at one low moment for one of the characters, they considered having an affair. While she was explaining this to her friend, her friend replied with something like, "Nothing you do could change what I think of you, that you are a good person." She was espousing the popular worldview that we can somehow create a dichotomy between *what we do* and *who we are*. But Jesus said the opposite is true: who we are determines what we do.

> For no good tree bears bad fruit, nor again does a bad tree bear good fruit, for each tree is known by its own fruit. For figs are not gathered from thorn bushes, nor are grapes picked from a bramble bush. The good person out of the good treasure of his heart produces good, and the evil person out of his evil treasure produces evil, for out of the abundance of the heart his mouth speaks (Luke 6:43–45).

Our own deceitfulness and hypocrisy is evident when we fail to apply the same standard to others. We are quick to deny that what we do is a reflection of who we are when we do wrong, but when someone wrongs or offends us, we are so quick to point out that *they* are "a bad person" because of what they've done. We also abandon our false-dichotomy when we do "good," and are quick to use it as an example that we are really "good people." However, Jesus says that "No one is good but God" (Mark 10:18).

The result of being "bad" people is that we are under God's wrath. Our greatest need for rescue is rescue *from* God. And the only one who can rescue us *is* God. As Christians, we must meditate regularly on the helpless and hopeless condition Jesus Christ has saved us from.

As a result of the depth of our sin, not only are we under God's judgement, but we are totally unable to do anything about it. We don't *want* to do anything about it. This means that we cannot save ourselves. How does God respond to such sin? How does God respond to our spiritual deadness? He responds in love, with grace.

The cause of salvation by grace alone:
The great love of God (v. 4)
Salvation is not a response of God to our works, goodness, or love, but rather, the overflow of his love for lost sinners. Salvation by grace alone displays the riches of God's love. "But God" (v. 4) are two of the most encouraging words in the Bible. They signal that God is going to step in himself and do something about our desperate estate. And why does he step in? Is it because we are lovable? Is it because we first sought him? Is it because of anything owing to us? No. It is simply because of his great love for us. According to Scripture,

God's love is most clearly displayed in his love for those who do not love him:

> For while we were still weak, at the right time Christ died for the ungodly. For one will scarcely die for a righteous person—though perhaps for a good person one would dare even to die—but God shows his love for us in that while we were still sinners, Christ died for us (Rom. 5:6-8)

Paul's point is this: God's love is unique in that it is demonstrated towards people who do not love him— people like us weak sinners. Maybe, just maybe, someone will love the lovable, and give their life for a good person. But God, in contrast, shows his love in dying for bad people. This is grace. John spoke of God's love in the same way: "In this is love, not that we have loved God but that he loved us and sent his Son to be the propitiation for our sins" (1 Jn. 4:10).

In short, to distort God's grace is to distort His love. In a sad irony, many feel compelled to maintain the notion that God somehow responds to our "loveliness" in order to help people "feel loved." The underlying presupposition is, "True love must love me for who I am." But the biblical picture of God and his love is far superior: God loves us *in spite of who we are.* He does not respond to our loveliness, but his love is what makes us lovely (cf. Eph. 5:25-28). One of the greatest tragedies of ignoring or downplaying the desperate, rebellious, powerless states of sinners apart from God's grace is that it *minimizes the love of God.*

The gracious work of God in salvation (vv. 4–10)
The work of God in salvation is the perfect remedy for our condition, and a display of His grace. In Christ, we have resurrection from death—spiritual, and one day, physical. We have freedom from the enslaving influences of the world, the flesh, and the devil. And we have forgiveness instead of condemnation for the penalty our sin deserves.

First, notice that all of the blessings of salvation come to us *in Christ*. It is the Lord Jesus Christ who has done the work of salvation. We are united to *him* by faith, and all that his life, death and resurrection accomplished become ours. To be saved by Grace alone is to be saved by *Christ* alone, for Christ is the grace of God that has appeared bringing salvation to all men (Titus 2:11). He is grace personified; the supreme display of the grace of God.

This is the most important point to grasp in understanding the biblical doctrine of the grace of God: that grace is not a *thing*, but ultimately, Jesus Christ. God does not simply impart grace to us as something distinct from himself, but rather gives himself in the person of Jesus Christ. Practically, grace is not some "spiritual strength" we are given to jump-start our dead batteries. It is not some pre-conversion power we add to our own works and strength to increase our receptivity to Christ. Indeed, the battle of the Reformation was really a battle over the word *alone*. To form a theology of grace that is something distinct from Christ is to distort grace. Further, this allows for grace to be something "added" to our works. But to receive grace *is* to receive Christ. This also demonstrates the inseparability of the solas: to be saved by grace alone is to be saved by Christ alone, through faith alone.

Paul writes that we have been 'made alive together with Christ' and 'raised' with him. That is, we have been resurrected from spiritual death to spiritual life. Carl Truman comments appropriately on this reality, writing:

> We do not need spiritual healing, for that would imply we are merely in need of repair. We need spiritual resurrection. And resurrection is the unilateral act of God, not a cooperative exercise between the living God and the dead. That is vital for an accurate understanding of grace. Grace is not God giving wholesome advice of a helping hand. It is God raising someone from the dead, first Christ and then those who are in Christ.[15]

Next, we see that we have been made a 'new creation.' If the problem is our very nature, we need a new nature. We need to be made into a new creation. This is precisely what Paul says God has done in our lives if we are united to Christ: "For we are his workmanship, created in Christ Jesus for good works, which God prepared beforehand, that we should walk in them" (Eph. 2:10).

In the Kingdom of God there are no 'self-made' men. As the Psalmist writes, there are only people God makes, by his grace: "Know that the Lord, he is God! It is he who made us, and not we ourselves; we are his people, and the sheep of his pasture" (Ps. 100:3).

We did not create ourselves, and we cannot recreate ourselves. It is the gracious work of God alone. This

---

[15] Carl Truman. *Grace Alone: Salvation as a Gift of God,* Ed. Matthew Barrett (Grand Rapids, MI: Zondervan, 2017), 41.

resurrection and new creation in Christ brings freedom from the things we were enslaved to. We are given new hearts and a new nature. We are born again (cf. John 3).

Lastly, when Paul writes that we have been "saved" (vv. 5, 8), he means we have been saved *from* the wrath of God. How? In Christ. The wrath of God was poured out on him at the cross, where he was the "propitiation for our sins" (1 Jn. 4:10). We could not repay God or make up for our sins. They must be punished. Christ, instead of us, was punished. As Paul says, "For our sake he made him to be sin who knew no sin, so that in him we might become the righteousness of God" (2 Cor. 5:21). He was raised from the dead, and us with him.

The goal of salvation by grace alone:
The praise of God's glorious Grace (v. 7)
Thus far we have considered how salvation by grace alone silences human self-exaltation and boasting. However, this not the ultimate goal of God in salvation, but rather, a necessary step towards that goal. The goal of God in salvation is the praise of his glory. Why does God save his people by grace? Paul tells us: "...so that in the coming ages he might show the immeasurable riches of his grace in kindness toward us in Christ Jesus" (v. 7). Why, in the ages to come, will God put "the immeasurable riches of his grace" on display? Paul tells us earlier in his letter:

> In love he predestined us for adoption to himself as sons through Jesus Christ, according to the purpose of his will, to the praise of his glorious grace, with which he has blessed us in the Beloved (Eph. 1:4-6).

The purpose of God *showing* the immeasurable riches of his grace is that his glorious grace would be *praised*. As we have already seen, God's grace is supremely revealed in Jesus Christ. To praise God's glorious grace is to praise God himself, which is why Paul says in verse 12 of chapter 1 that God's purpose in our salvation is the praise of his glory. We see his glory most fully in the person and work of Jesus Christ (2 Cor. 4:4-6). Thus, when we praise God's glorious grace or his glory, we are praising *him*.

This explains, coming full circle, why God works our salvation in such a way that cuts the root of self-exaltation and human boasting. Human boasting is essentially ascribing glory to others for what God alone should be glorified for. God has worked our salvation in such a way that he *alone* is glorified (*soli Deo gloria*). Salvation by grace alone through faith alone in Christ alone is how God alone receives glory. Here is our greatest argument and motivation for a continued articulation and defense of the doctrine of salvation by grace alone: the glory of God.

Conclusion

The Church of Jesus Christ desperately needs to recover the radical nature of Salvation by grace alone, through faith alone, in Christ alone, according to Scripture alone, to the glory of God alone. We need to hold up the clarifying-light of Scripture to the confusion of human experience, exposing the depth of our fall and the magnitude of our need. It is only in the Scriptures that we find the true description of our condition. This is not an end in itself, in the same way a diagnosis is not the treatment. But we will never understand God or ourselves, or appreciate His grace until we understand our total *need*. We need to recognize that part of mankind's lost condition is the proclivity towards self-exaltation and boasting. These qualities make us blind and resistant to the grace of God in Jesus Christ. Since this is a part of our fallen condition, we will always have to be defending *sola gratia*; not merely as an exercise of historical theology, but as an application of the gospel *today*. Until Jesus returns, sinful man will continue to exalt himself, and the light of the gospel will be needed to expose the darkness of our condition, and the source of our hope: Christ. Lastly, we must continue to be personally shaped by the grace of God. This will bear the fruit of humility, joy, and patience in our prayer and our ministry of the word.

Soli Deo Gloria.

6

GLORY ALONE

Rylan R. P. Auger

In 1538, the Italian Cardinal James Sadolet sought, by way of a letter, to persuade the Genevan Protestants to return to the Roman Catholic church. It was John Calvin's response, given in 1539, which first identified him as a Reformer across the European stage.[1] As it serves the purpose of this chapter, Calvin's letter gets to the heart of the Reformer's problem with the Catholic church. While commending Sadolet ever so graciously for his intellect and zeal, Calvin correctly assessed that such a zeal for justification by works, "keeps a man entirely devoted to himself, and does not, even by one expression, arouse him to sanctify the name of God." [2] He

---

[1] John Piper, *John Calvin and His Passion for the Majesty of God* (Wheaton: Crossway Books, 2009), 15.
[2] John Calvin, "Reply by Calvin to Cardinal Sadolet's Letter" in *John Calvin: Selections from His Writings* (Atlanta: Scholars Press, 1975), 89.

writes further, "it is not very sound theology, to confine a man's thoughts so much to himself, and not to set before him, as the prime motive of his existence, zeal to illustrate the glory of God. For we are born first of all for God, and not for ourselves. As all things flowed from him, and [exist] in him, so...they ought to be referred to him."[3] To rephrase Calvin: As we uphold justification by the grace of God alone, in the work of Christ alone, received by means of faith alone, taught on the basis of Scripture alone, so also we must do all things to *the glory of God alone. Soli Deo Gloria* is the primary motive of our lives as Christians.

At the heart of the Reformation was not a theological squabble over particulars. It was a protest for the glory of God to be given all rightful praise. It was not merely a zeal to *illustrate* the glory of God that drove these Reformers to fight back against the tyranny of the Catholic church—some of them at the cost of their very lives—but rather, to *know* the glory of God, to taste the joys of his person, and to be with him where he is. And they realized that to lose justification by faith was to lose their reward. To depart from justification by faith was to depart from the very glory of God. As Calvin went on to write in his reply to Sadolet: "where the knowledge of justification by faith is taken away, the glory of Christ is extinguished." Without justification by faith we are all helplessly dead in our sins and miserably separated from the glory of God.

---

[3] John Calvin, *John Calvin: Selections from His Writings,* 89.

The only way for us to have our reward, to be free from the weight of legal works and to be welcomed into the presence of God's glory, is to throw ourselves onto the gospel of justification by faith, and to be driven in all things to praise the glory of God alone. I want to show these things from Scripture by answering three questions: 1) What is the glory of God? 2) How is God glorified through our salvation? 3) Why is his glory so praiseworthy?

What is The Glory of God?
Only God's words could rightly define his glory. That's why we must let Scripture be the authority on such matters, *sola scriptura*, so that we do not dishonour the glory of God. Moreover, there's a sense in which describing glory itself is impossible. I mean that, it is impossible in the same way that I cannot explain to you what beauty is. I can merely point at enough things that are considered beautiful until you begin to grasp the concept.[4] So it is with the glory of God. Glory is not defined, glory is seen. I can only point us to the ways in Scripture that God has shown us his glory. Of course, in this short chapter, we would never be able to behold all of the glory displayed for us in the Scripture, but let us aim to answer our question as sufficiently as possible.

What God reveals to us in Scripture is this: *The glory of God is seen in who God is and what God does.*

---

[4] John Piper, "To Him Be glory Forevermore," Sermon, Bethlehem Baptist Church, December 17, 2006.

This is what Moses sees when he asks God in Exodus 33, "Show me your glory." Listen to how God first responds to Moses's request: "I will make all my goodness pass before you and I will proclaim before you my name, 'The Lord' and I will be gracious to whom I will be gracious, and I will be merciful to whom I will be merciful" (Ex. 33:19).

God essentially tells Moses that he will see two things when his glory passes by: his name, the LORD (who God is), and that he is going to act in accordance with his will (what God does). And a few verses later God does exactly this, but we get more details. He proclaims His name, saying, "The LORD, the LORD, a God merciful and gracious, slow to anger and abounding in steadfast love and faithfulness, keeping steadfast love for thousands, forgiving iniquity and transgression and sin, but who will by no means clear the guilty visiting the sins of the father on the children and the children's children. And Moses quickly bowed his head toward the earth and worshiped" (Ex. 34:6-8).

God's revelation here shows is that his glory is:
1) Who he is, via his name explicitly: "The LORD (*yhwh*) God most high" has a personal name; he is no mere abstraction, but he has personhood.
2) Who he is, via his character intrinsically: He is a God merciful and gracious, slow to anger, and abounding in steadfast love and faithfulness.
3) What he does, via his actions: He shows steadfast love to thousands, forgiving sin, and executing justice on the guilty.

In summary, we see God's glory in his name and in his ways. It's who he is intrinsically and what he does accordingly. Specifically, we see that God is gracious and merciful, loving and faithful, and forgiving of sins, yet God is just, rightly punishing the guilty. This is an incredible proclamation, but if we were to stop here we would not yet fully comprehend the glory of God. And we are not meant to stop here.

Moses had seen the Lord miraculously plague Egypt and part the sea to rescue his people. He saw a manifestation of God's glory in the cloud bringing the law, but after all that he still asks, "Show me your glory", because he knew there was more to see. Even though this revelation of God's glory caused Moses to bow his head and worship, we know there must be more, because there is an unexplained tension between God who forgives and God who will by no means clear the guilty. The problem is that we are guilty!

Now, you may ask how can we know we are sinners under God's wrath if we have never heard of God before. The answer is that everyone has heard of God. They have seen in creation the voice that is crying out the glory of God. "The heavens declare the glory of God…there is no speech, nor are there words, whose voice is not heard" (Ps. 19:1, 3). Everyone in all the world who has ever simply looked up to the sky has seen the glory of God. The implication is not that the sky is the final testimony, but that as creatures of the creator, we know that he exists. Paul picks up this idea from the Psalms, and goes on to say that we all know that there is wrath coming for those who do not worship him; because we can clearly see his divine nature and eternal power in creation, we are "without excuse" (Rom 1:20). He says we "have exchanged the glory of the immortal God for images...they worshiped and served the creature rather than the Creator, who is blessed forever" (Rom. 1:23, 25). So because we can clearly see that he deserves to be worshiped, everyone, all humans are held accountable to the fact that we have not worshiped him in his glory. We are all sinners under God's wrath. "All have sinned and fallen short of the glory of God" (Rom. 3:23). "There is no one righteous not one" (Psalm 14:1).

So we return to our problem: How can God punish my sin, and yet forgive it?

The continued revelation of Scripture is necessary for us to answer these questions and truly see his glory. Exodus is not enough. The whole Old Testament is not enough. We can only fully see who God is and what he does by looking at the person and work of Christ. This is why Peter tells us, "we have the prophetic word more fully confirmed" referring to the appearing of God's Son (2 Peter 1:19). Now that Jesus has come, we see the confirmation, the clarification, of the Old Testament.

We see this clearly in 2 Corinthians chapters 3-4, where Paul picks up the idea of the glory Moses saw and explains that there is a glory that surpasses it (2 Cor. 3:7-18). In fact, Paul suggests that those who are still looking back at the partial display of glory as though it were the fullest are, in reality, completely blind to God's glory. He says, "To this day, when they read the old covenant, that same veil remains unlifted, because *only through Christ* is it taken away" (2 Cor. 3:14). Paul explains further that they are blind to "the light of the gospel of the glory of Christ, who is the image of God" (2 Cor. 4:4). He then re-words this by saying, "For God, who said 'let light shine out of darkness,' has shone in our hearts to give the light of the knowledge of the glory of God in the face of Jesus Christ" (4:6). Again, they cannot see God's glory because God must show it to them; they refuse to see it because in unbelief they do not look to the person of Christ.

Jesus is the fullest revelation of God's glory. He is the image of God. He shows us exactly who God is and what he is like. And in these verses, Paul wants us to understand explicitly that when Jesus shows us what God is like he is in fact showing us the very glory of God. That is why he says we are given "the knowledge of God's glory in the face of Jesus Christ." He also wants us to know specifically that Christ has shown God's glory to us through the gospel.[5] Thus he says, "the light of the *gospel* of the glory of Christ."

If you look at who Jesus is and what Jesus has done, you'll see who God is and you'll see what God does. John

---

[5] Paul uses the idea of light to explain both our seeing and our understanding. Unbelievers do not see the light of the gospel of the glory of Christ. That's the negative way of saying it. The positive way is that believers have been shown by God the light of the knowledge of his glory in the face of Christ. On the one hand, we see it by looking at the gospel; we see it in the face of Jesus. On the other hand, we understand it only by the gracious revelation of God.

tells us, "We have seen his glory, glory as of the only Son from the Father, full of grace and truth" (Jn. 1:14). When you see who Christ is in the gospel, only then will you see God's glory clearly. *Sola Christus*. Jesus says, "when you have lifted up the Son of Man, then you will know that I am he, and that I do nothing on my own authority, but I speak just as the Father taught me" (John 8:28).

And it's only in the gospel of the glory of Christ that we understand the glory God proclaimed to Moses in Exodus. It's in Christ that we see a loving gracious, merciful, patient, and just God. In the gospel, God's mercy and justice are fully upheld and wonderfully displayed. That's why Paul in Romans 3:24-25 tell us, "we are justified by grace as a gift, through the redemption that is in Christ Jesus, whom God put forward as a propitiation by his blood, to be received by faith. This was to show God's righteousness, because in his divine forbearance he had passed over former sins." What in Exodus seemed to be a contradiction is here in Jesus the source of all our hope. All God's wrath towards guilty sinners who dishonor him, who do not trust him, who refuse to enjoy him, is punished in Jesus on the cross. The price has been paid, and God's mercy and forgiveness are purchased at the cross by his gracious sacrifice. One and the same: sin punished, sinners forgiven. But who could pay such a weighty price, who could divert so weighty a punishment? None other than God alone. The great surprise of God's glory is that his grace, mercy, and love are displayed not just in any substitute payment for our sins, but in his taking that very cost upon himself in the body of Christ crucified for us.

In summary, God's glory, who he is and what he does, is to be the saviour of sinners in Christ Jesus, and to rescue them by dying in their place. That is the picture drawn out for us in Scripture. That is why the author of Hebrews can assert simply and directly that Christ is, "the radiance of the glory of God, and the exact imprint of his nature, and he upholds the universe by the word of his power. After making purification for sins, he sat down at the right hand of the Majesty on high" (Heb. 1:3).

Why is God Glorified Through Our Salvation?

We've already seen from Scripture that God has chosen to display his glory in the person and work of Jesus Christ, and that our salvation comes on the basis of justification by faith. But now we must ask ourselves: Why should a holy God see fit to glorify himself in this particular way of salvation for sinners? Why should he reveal his glory through our justification by faith?

We could answer simply, "because that's how he manifests his glory for us. Justification by faith is the display of his gracious mercy and justice in the person and work of Christ." But God does not merely display his glory, God saves us to exalt his glory. In other words, the ultimate reason God saves us through justification by faith is for the praise of His glory. Indeed, praise for His glory is the ultimate reason

God does all things. God is radically driven by this purpose in everything he does, and particularly so in salvation.

Consider: "For my name's sake I defer my anger, for the sake of my praise I restrain it for you, that I may not cut you off...For my own sake, for my own sake, I do it, for how should my name be profaned? My glory I will not give to another" (Is. 48:9,11). God's purpose in rescuing from his judgment, in redeeming us from our sin, is to get praise for his name, for his glory. Remember that God's name is who God is and what God does. God is not going to allow anyone to steal praise for who he is and what he has done. God will not share his glory, meaning he will not let anyone else receive the praise which he alone deserves. In fact, to praise someone other than God for our salvation would profane his name, it would dishonour him.

We understand the idea that God alone deserves praise for what is due to his character, because we would never praise someone else for things we have done. Or perhaps, we understand that if a man were to give praise to another woman for the love his wife shows to him, he would not be honouring his wife for who she is and what she does. A more fitting analogy for those of my younger generation might be the participation ribbon. We love to give out ribbons to everyone who participates, but the participation ribbon steals the rightful glory the victor! And moreover (as someone who has received a lot of participation ribbons), there is no genuine reward to be found in receiving praise we did not earn. So let's not deprive God of the praise he alone deserves.

And he deserves all our praise, "For from him and to him and through him are all things. To him be glory forever. Amen" (Rom. 11:36). Allow me to quote a lengthier passage from Ephesians where this is emphasized:

> Blessed be the God and Father of our Lord Jesus Christ, who has blessed us in Christ with every spiritual blessing in the heavenly places, even as he chose us in him before the foundation of the world that we should be holy and blameless before him. In love he predestined us for adoption as sons through Jesus Christ *according to the pleasure of his will, to the praise of the glory of his grace*, which he has freely given us in the beloved one. In him we have the redemption through his blood, the forgiveness of trespasses, according to the riches of his grace, which he lavished upon us in all wisdom and insight making known to us the mystery of his will, according to his pleasure, which he set forth in Christ as a plan for the fullness of time, to bring unity to all things in heaven and on earth under Christ. In him we have obtained an inheritance, having been predestined according to the plan of him who *works all things according to the counsel of his will*, so that we who were the first to hope in Christ might be *to the praise of his glory*. In him you also, when you heard the word of truth, the gospel of your salvation, and believed in him, were sealed with the promised Holy Spirit, who is the guarantee of our

inheritance until we acquire possession of it *to the praise of his glory* (Eph. 1:3-14, emphasis added).

As we read through this text it is abundantly clear that God's one ultimate goal is the praise of his glory. We see this phrase repeated three times. Paul first explains "he predestined us for adoption as sons through Christ Jesus according to the pleasure of his will, to *the praise of the glory of his grace*" (1:5-6). Now we don't see the words justification or salvation in this text, but we do see that we are talking about all the benefits of salvation that we have in Christ. Election, adoption, redemption, reconciliation, and our inheritance. And the goal of them all is for God to get praise for his glory.

Verses 11-12 emphasize that this is the ultimate purpose of God: "We have been predestined according to plan of God who works all things according to the counsel of his will, so that we who were the first to hope in Christ might be *to the praise of his glory*." Salvation is included in the "all things" which God is working towards for the goal of getting praise for his glory. So God's ultimate purpose in all things is praise for his glory, but we see that salvation, namely our justification by faith, is particularly to the praise of his glory.

We could summarize it this way: God displays his glory through Christ, so that the blessings of his glory given to us in salvation would result in our praising him.

Now, before moving one form this, I want to point out a particular reason in which salvation through justification by faith is God's chosen means to display his glory. Getting praise for his glory is the ultimate reason, but the particular reason is to make us depend on his sovereign grace. Or we could say, so that we would not depend on ourselves at all, not even one inkling.

Throughout this passage the manner of God's actions are always based solely on his own purpose and will and nothing else. And these plans and purposes are always the overflow of his good pleasure and his grace. Remember, "in love he predestined us...according to his pleasure, to the praise of the glory of his grace, which he has freely given us in the beloved." He saved us because it pleased him to, he wanted to. And it wasn't because he saw something in us that he wanted to get, but he wants to give something freely to us. *Sola gratia.* If we skip ahead to we see Paul say it explicitly: "For by grace you have been saved through faith. And this is not of your own doing; it is a gift of God, not a result of works, so that no one may boast" (Eph. 2:8). The particular reason that God has saved us through our justification by faith is that when it comes time praise the one who accomplished it, everything is pointing to God. As Paul says when he looks back on God's interactions in Exodus 33: "For he says to Moses, 'I will have mercy on whom I have mercy and I will have compassion on whom I have compassion.' So then it depends not on human will or exertion, but on God, who shows mercy" (Rom 9:15-16). God is working in all things to get praise. Therefore, salvation is completely dependent on his will and his grace. We have no boast in ourselves, but let the one who boasts, boast in the Lord (1 Cor. 1:31).

What Compels Us To Praise God For His Glory?

If God gets praise for his glory, what does that mean for us? Why does it matter if we uphold justification by grace alone, in Christ alone, through faith alone, on the basis of Scripture alone, to the glory of God alone?

We are compelled to praise God's glory because He gets praise for his glory through our joy in himself. Thus, we delight to do all things to the praise of God's glory alone because he is most glorified in our delight in him.[6] God's zealousness for the praise of his glory is a zealousness for the joy of his people. They are not opposed to one another. The praise of God's glory is accomplished through our happiness.

Look again at Ephesians 1:3. Did you notice that Paul doesn't begin with explaining his theology, or even demanding that we worship God? He's not giving logical premises and conclusions; he's overflowing in praise! He opens with the phrase "Blessed be the God and Father of our Lord Jesus Christ, who has blessed us." Essentially, Paul says, "Praise be to God, for getting *his* praise through *my* joy."

Genuine praise is the completion of happiness. Or we could say, happiness climaxes when it overflows in praise. C.S. Lewis explains it this way: "We delight to praise what we enjoy because praise not merely expresses but completes the enjoyment; it is its appointed consummation."[7] If you enjoy watching sports, you can probably recall how natural it

---

[6] See John Piper, *Desiring God* (Wheaton: Crossway, 1986).

[7] C.S. Lewis, *Reflections on the Psalms* (London: Harper Collins, 1998), 77–84.

feels to not merely enjoy the sport but to praise the things which you enjoy about it. Or perhaps you enjoyed the movie you saw last week; watching the film was enjoyable, but you want to tell someone about it. Or if you have kids, you know you delight in them, yet you feel the need to tell them that you love them. Praise is the natural completion of our enjoyment.

Jonathan Edwards says it this way: "God is glorified not only by his glory being seen, but by its being rejoiced in. When those that see it delight in it, God is more glorified than if they only see it. His glory is then received by the whole soul, both by the understanding and by the heart."[8]

We must not merely see the glory of God, but rejoice in it, rejoice in him, praise him. This joy only comes through salvation in Christ when we see the glory of God in the face of Jesus.

Lewis himself demonstrates how he could not see the praiseworthiness of God before he had been justified in Christ.[9] Before his conversion, he thought that God in the Psalms sounds like a vain old lady demanding compliments all the time, "Praise me, praise me, praise me!" But after coming to Christ, when Lewis realized that God was the greatest source of joy, praise for God was simply the natural

---

[8] Jonathan Edwards, *The "Miscellanies"*, in *The Works of Jonathan Edwards*, vol. 13, ed. Thomas Schafer (New Haven: Yale University Press, 1994), 495, Miscellany #448, Emphasis added. Cited in *The Supremacy of God in Preaching*, John Piper, 11-12.

[9] Ibid., 80.

response, not a coercion. If praise does not flow out of enjoyment, it ceases to be genuine praise. It's vain flattery. This is why God says, "This people honours me with their lips, but their heart is far from me" (Is. 29:13). To praise God apart from genuine delight in him is not genuine praise.

Perhaps we ought to look at the Psalms themselves to see the union of God's praise and our joy. David says in Psalm 92: "It is good to give thanks to God, to sing praises to the most high...*because* you, O Lord, have made me glad by your work; at the works of your hands I sing for joy" (emphasis added). God's glory makes us glad. Our joy in him is the basis of our praise.

When we enjoy him, we don't separate his works, his character, or his glory from him. This is important. We fully see his glory in the person and work of Jesus, so we can only truly enjoy the glory of God in the person of Jesus. The glory of God is no abstraction. To enjoy his glory is to enjoy him. To praise his glory is to praise him.

So why is God so worthy of our praise? That is to say, why are we so compelled to praise God for his glory? God is worthy of our eternal praise because he is the source of eternal joy. Through the death and resurrection of Christ, God has made "known to us the path of life, in [his] presence there is fullness of joy; at [his] right hand are pleasures forevermore" (Ps. 16:11).

Martin Luther spoke of his encounter with salvation in Christ by faith in this way: "At last, by the mercy of God, meditating day and night...I began to understand that the righteousness of God is that by which the righteous live by a gift of God, namely by faith...Here I felt that I was altogether born again and had entered paradise itself through open gates."[10] What an amazing declaration. The news of his salvation in Christ was for Luther the entrance into paradise itself. For us, there are two applications here, one negative and one positive.

Negatively, if we abandon justification by faith, we not only totally destroy the basis of our joy, but we greatly dishonour the glory of God. As we earlier noted Calvin as saying, "where the knowledge of justification by faith is taken away, the glory of Christ is extinguished." This is why the Reformers strove to preserve these doctrines and the authority of Scripture. They did all for the glory of God, and their joy in him. If we want to have our deepest joy, we must maintain, witness, and live out the reality that God has accomplished our complete salvation by his grace alone, and through faith we become receivers of it.

Positively then, "whether we eat or drink", we can and must "do all things to the glory of God" (1 Cor 10:31), without the fear that we are sacrificing our happiness. In seeking to praise God for his glory we are thereby necessarily receiving joy in him. It's very important that we do not seek our joy above seeking the praise of his glory. We won't be

---

[10] Martin Luther, "Preface to the Complete Edition of Luther's Latin Writings", in *Martin Luther: Selections from His Writings,* ed. John Dillenberger (New York: Random House Inc., 1962), 11.

satisfied apart from God, but in God's glory alone will we find our ultimate joy.

Summary

What is the glory of God? Jesus is the radiance of God's glory, we see who God is, in what Christ has done for us. *Why is God glorified in our salvation?* Because the ultimate purpose of God is to receive praise for his glory. *Why is his glory worthy of praise?* Because our joy in God's glory, in God himself, naturally overflows in His praise.

Soli Deo Gloria is not merely a Reformation principal. It's the cry of all creation, for all eternity. The day is coming when God will return, and every knee will bow and every tongue confess, whether submissively under the power of his justice, or willingly in delightful praise, that Jesus Christ is Lord, to the glory of God alone.

7

SEMPER REFORMANDA:

Always being reformed according to the Word of God

Alexander Kloosterman

Why did we think it would be good to do a conference on the Reformation? The purpose of this conference is not only to consider the Reformation as an historical event, but also, to consider what impact the work of God in the past should have on our lives *now*. We believe that the Reformation was no less than the return to Scripture and the recovery of the gospel for the church and the world. We believe the five *Solas*, which are helpful summaries of the teaching of the reformers, are really summaries of the Christian gospel. Therefore, this gospel that was recovered should be taking root and bearing fruit in our churches today. In other words, we don't want this to be a bare history lesson of events in the past, which we passively admire from a distance. Our aim is that the light of the gospel would shine brightly again into our own lives and churches.

How would we know if the light of the gospel was penetrating our lives and world? What would the be the impact of such illumination? The evidence of that light, as this talk will seek to demonstrate, is that our lives will constantly be reforming to the Word of God and the gospel.

One way the church has, in the past, described a life and ministry shaped by the gospel is through the phrase *semper reformanda*, or "always being reformed." To put it into biblical categories, it will be a life of faith and repentance.

Michael Horton writes that the term, "semper reformanda" first appeared in a 1674 devotional written by a Dutch man named Jodocus van Lodenstein. The full phrase was, "The church is reformed and always [in need of] being reformed according to the Word of God."[1] Horton makes an important observation regarding the meaning of this phrase. He writes, "The verb is passive: the church is not "always reforming," but is "always being reformed" by the Spirit of God through the Word."[2] It is the Spirit working through the Word that the true church of Jesus Christ is being reformed; not ultimately to a system of doctrine, but "conformed to the image of Christ" (Rom. 8:29). He is the substance and goal of our teaching.

All of this Latin talk might be making you suspicious. Why, you might ask, are we speaking in language and categories I haven't read in my Bible? That is a good question, and I want to put this helpful phrase into biblical categories. I believe a life that is "always being reformed according to the Word of God" is what the Bible refers to as a life of "faith and repentance." It is a summary of the substance of the Christian life; one of faith in the Son of God, and repentance unto Him. A truly reformed life is not one that remains static, but one that is constantly being reformed.

---

[1] Michael Horton, "Semper Reformation". In *Tabletalk Magazine*, October 1, 2009 https://www.ligonier.org/learn/articles/semper-reformanda/(accessed October 2017).

[2] Horton, Semper Reformation.

Semper Reformanda Does Not Mean "Always Changing"
In our current cultural climate, change for change-sake is often considered inherently good. Slap the term "progressive" onto a group or set of values, and they seem to automatically inherit moral superiority. To say that you are progressive, generally, is to say that you are "moving in the right moral direction.", leaving behind what is bad and moving forward towards what is good. The reason this progressive language has moral weight is that large portions of society have accepted the idea that the past is inherently bad, and the future is inherently good. Wildly successful political campaigns have been run on a single word: *change.*

That is why people can use the threat of being on the "wrong side of history" when talking about moral issues. The assumption is, society is "progressing" morally, and you don't want to be left behind. The important takeaway from all of this is that, according to this worldview, *change* is inherently good.

This is not true, and this is *not* what *semper reformanda* means. It does not mean that the church should always be willing to change for change sake. It means *the church should always be willing to walk in faith and repentance, according to the Word of God.* The church should always be willing to examine itself according to the revelation of Jesus Christ in Scripture, and to turn to Him in faith and repentance. This may mean changing. And it may mean holding fast.

This is, in fact, a deeply biblical teaching. A church that is not being reformed according to the Word of God is not, in fact, a church.

Always in Need of Being Reformed:
A Life of Faith and Repentance

Faith and repentance are not 'higher level' skills or traits that particularly mature Christians possess, but the marks of every true believer. The first of Martin Luther's 95 states "When our Lord and Master Jesus Christ said, 'Repent' (Mt. 4:17), he willed the entire life of believers to be one of repentance." This is significant. I think by "the entire life of believers" he meant both that every *area* of their life is committed to repentance, and that for the entire *length* of their life.

Our Lord and Master Jesus Christ calls Christians to repent in every area of their life, for all of their life. This means that if there is an area of our life that does not align with Scripture, we must repent, that is turn from it, and then turn to Christ by faith.

Faith and repentance are inseparable
According to Scripture, faith and repentance are inseparable - they are like two sides to the same coin. We see this clearly in Mark 1:4–15:

> Now after John was arrested, Jesus came into Galilee, proclaiming the gospel of God, and saying, "The time is fulfilled, and the kingdom of God is at hand; *repent and believe in the gospel"* (Mark 1:14–15, emphasis added).

In Paul's sermon at Athens, he says, "The times of ignorance God overlooked, but now he commands all people everywhere to repent," and the result was that, "some men joined him and believed" (Acts 17:30, 34). The repentance that God commanded, and the belief of those who heard the gospel, were inseparable. When God calls a man to faith, he calls him to repentance.

John Murray rightly concluded, "The faith that is unto salvation is a penitent faith and the repentance that is unto life is a believing repentance...it is impossible to disentangle faith and repentance. Saving faith is permeated with repentance and repentance is permeated with faith."[3]

All of life should be a life of faith and repentance
The Scriptures also teach that the whole of the Christian life should be characterized by faith and repentance:

> I have been crucified with Christ. It is no longer I who live, but Christ who lives in me. And the life I now live in the flesh I live by faith in the Son of God, who loved me and gave himself for me (Gal. 2:20).

Faith is not something we receive at a certain moment in time, and then leave behind as we get to the *real* work of the Christian life. Paul is essentially saying that every step and every breath we take is to be done in faith—"the life I now live in the flesh I live by faith." In other words, the Christian's every waking moment is to be lived out in faith. Since all of life must be a life of faith, so too all of life must be a life of repentance.

This means that, until we see Jesus face-to-face, and are transformed fully into his image, we must constantly be turning from our sin, and turning to Him in faith.

Sin is an ongoing reality of our experience

---

[3] John Murray, *Redemption Accomplished and Applied* (Grand Rapids, MI:Wm. B. Eerdmans Publishing Co, 1955), 113.

The reality is that Christians, although new creatures, are still sinful, and so stand in constant need of faith and repentance. Jesus himself taught us to pray everyday: "Give us this day our daily bread, and forgive us our debts, as we also have forgiven our debtors (Matthew 6:11-12). That means that every morning we wake up and ask the question - what do I need today? And the answer is that we need bread to sustain us, and forgiveness for our daily sin.

Denying we are sinful is evidence we don't have faith
Throughout the history of the church, people have attempted to downplay or deny the fact that, for the Christian, sin remains. However, far from a means to freedom, this teaching is a lie. To deny that we are sinful and in need of daily grace is to deny God's word:

> If we say we have no sin, we deceive ourselves, and the truth is not in us. If we confess our sins, he is faithful and just to forgive us our sins and to cleanse us from all unrighteousness. If we say we have not sinned, we make him a liar, and his word is not in us (1 Jn. 1:8-10).

The true evidence of our Christian maturity is that we have an ever-deepening awareness of our need for grace. A denial of our sin is a functional denial of our own need for God's grace and transforming power in our lives. Faith believes God's word regarding who He is and who we are, and trusts Christ for all He has promised to be to us. Denying our sin is saying to God, "you are not right about me."

Faith and repentance in every area of our lives
Faith and repentance are not only to be ongoing realities in our life, but they must be a reality in every *area* of our lives. Compartmentalization is the enemy of faith and repentance. It might be tempting to look at some suspicious practices of the catholic church and comfort ourselves in our orthodoxy, but we are not called to repent of other people's sins, but our own. Jesus himself confronts our tendency towards compartmentalizing. For example, in Mark 10 we see Jesus respond to an eager, but ignorant, young man:

> And as he was setting out on his journey, a man ran up and knelt before him and asked him, "Good Teacher, what must I do to inherit eternal life?" And Jesus said to him, "Why do you call me good? No one is good except God alone. You know the commandments: 'Do not murder, Do not commit adultery, Do not steal, Do not bear false witness, Do not defraud, Honor your father and mother.'" And he said to him, "Teacher, all these I have kept from my youth." And Jesus, looking at him, loved him, and said to him, "You lack one thing: go, sell all that you have and give to the poor, and you will have treasure in heaven; and come, follow me." Disheartened by the saying, he went away sorrowful, for he had great possessions (Mark 10:17-22).

The rich young man did not consider Jesus a greater treasure than the wealth he was told to give away. He had compartmentalized his life. He came to Jesus to tell him he had done everything right but then Jesus, because he loved him, exposed the one area of his life where he needed to exercise faith and repentance.

Are there areas of our own lives towards which we need to walk in repentance? Where are the habitual sins in our lives? What areas of service are we neglecting in our churches? The call of the reformation is not "look at everything bad out there, and how good we have it here," but "we all need to be submit ourselves to the Word of God." If we're honest, we will probably find many areas of our lives that need to come under the authority and light of the gospel. Those areas are precisely where Jesus calls us to follow him.

There is also another passage from Matthew:

> Whoever loves father or mother more than me is not worthy of me, and whoever loves son or daughter more than me is not worthy of me. And whoever does not take his cross and follow me is not worthy of me. Whoever finds his life will lose it, and whoever loses his life for my sake will find it (Mt. 10:37–39).

Jesus Christ calls us to faith and repentance in every area of our lives. We are called to love him and treasure him more than anything or anyone else. That is why compartmentalizing our lives is so dangerous. Where we are willing to pick up our cross in everything except "that", we must realize that "that" area of our lives is precisely where we must demonstrate faith and repentance.

Faith and repentance in light of all of Scripture
Another way we avoid faith and repentance is by ignoring or minimizing those portions of God's Word we find difficult.

But a truly "reforming" ministry is not just one that settles for faith and repentance according to certain parts of Scripture, but to all of it. Jesus himself pointed out this temptation towards hypocrisy:

> Woe to you, scribes and Pharisees, hypocrites! For you tithe mint and dill and cumin, and have neglected the weightier matters of the law: justice and mercy and faithfulness. These you ought to have done, without neglecting the others (Mt. 23:23).

Though they kept a portion of the law, the hypocrisy of the Pharisees was seen in their intentional neglect of the weightier matters of the law - justice, mercy, and faithfulness. None of us like to have the weakest things in our lives exposed to the light of Scripture, but until they are, we will be unable to walk in true repentance. Right doctrine, without heartfelt obedience, is little more than a husk - a form of godliness, devoid of any real power.

Source and Strength for Faith and Repentance

All of this may seem like an impossible task, and humanly speaking, it is. But it is not impossible for God (Matt 19:26). God is able to produce in us the faith and repentance He requires. We must always remember, however, that He does this through his *word*. To continually be seeking personal reformation means immersing ourselves in Scripture, because it is therein that we find the source and strength for obedience. "So faith comes from hearing, and hearing through the word of Christ" (Rom. 10:17). This verse tell us that it is the word of Christ which produces faith.

That means that even when a sinner, completely devoid of faith, sits under the Word, the Spirit can use it to awaken faith in them. When we compartmentalize parts of Scripture however, we are withholding part of Christ; we are robbing people of the means for faith.

Ultimately we must admit that any hope of true and lasting reformation is hopeless without the powerful working of God's grace, by his Spirit, through his Word. Faith is not conjured up in self-strength. It is the fruit of the Spirit working through the Word.

A Life of Humility and Unity
Humility

> But this is the one to whom I will look: he who is humble and contrite in spirit and trembles at my word (Is. 66:2);

Sometimes we talk about living a radical life, or having radical ministry. We want our churches to be effective, we want our personal lives to be effective. But what does God bless? Who does he look upon? He who is humble. And the true test of our humility is how we respond to the Word of God. On the ground then, someone who is "contrite in spirit and trembles at God's word" will have a high view of Scripture and constantly be holding up his own life to the light of Scripture, and ultimately to the Lord Jesus Christ. We find that this kind of humility leads to self-reflection:

> Why do you see the speck that is in your brother's eye, but do not notice the log that is in your own eye? Or how can you say to your brother, "Let me take

the speck out of your eye," when there is the log in your own eye? You hypocrite, first take the log out of your own eye, and then you will see clearly to take the speck out of your brother's eye (Mt. 7:3-5).

A life that is always being reformed is one that is characterized by the prioritization of humble self-reflection and repentance. We understand that the biggest problem we're going to face is *not* out there, but within our own hearts. The life of faith and repentance is a humble life, and one that examines itself first before others.

Unity
Secondly, a life lived in faith and repentance, will be a life that shares profound fellowship with other Christians who share our love for the same truths.

And he gave the apostles, the prophets, the evangelists, the shepherds and teachers, to equip the saints for the work of ministry, for building up the body of Christ, until we all attain to the unity of the faith and of the knowledge of the Son of God, to mature manhood, to the measure of the stature of the fullness of Christ, so that we may no longer be children, tossed to and fro by the waves and carried about by every wind of doctrine, by human cunning, by craftiness in deceitful schemes. Rather, speaking the truth in love, we are to grow up in every way into him who is the head, into Christ, from whom the whole body, joined and held together by every joint with which it is equipped, when each part is working properly, makes the body grow so that it builds itself up in love (Eph. 4:11-16);

Until we all attain to the unity of the faith and of the knowledge of the Son of God, to mature manhood, to the measure of the stature of the fullness of Christ (Eph. 4:13).

God's goal for his church is unity in the knowledge of the Son of God; in other words, true unity only comes about through the truth. Where there is no agreement on the nature and person of Jesus Christ, there can be no unity. Just as the Spirit worked through the Word to unify the church around the person and work of Jesus Christ in the days of the Reformation however, so too we believe he can do it again— That is our prayer.

So what does it mean to follow Jesus? It means living a life of faith and repentance; faith in all that Christ is, and all that He has done, and repentance from any obstacle to honoring him. The Church, and all Christians, are in constant need of renewal, to greater reflect the glory of Jesus Christ. The truly 'reformed' life is the one that is constantly being reformed according to the word of God, by the Spirit, through the Son, to the glory of the Father. May God do this work in our hearts.

Semper Reformanda.

8

WILLIAM TYNDALE

Derek Green

There's no *hard* evidence about him until he appeared in Oxford in his teens,[1] but it's believed that William Tyndale was born around the year 1494 in the region of Gloucestershire, England, and probably near the town of Dursle, between the Cotswold Hills to the east and the Severn River to the west.

In 1506, at probably twelve years of age, he moved to Oxford, about 50 miles away, to attend the Magdalen School. The school system he was entering was based on a philosophy of education that linked school, college, and university.[2] For Tyndale, this meant he would stay at Oxford for a total of nine years, graduating with a masters' degree sometime around 1515, at the age of 21.[3]

---

[1] David Daniell, *William Tyndale: A Biography* (New Haven: Yale University Pres, 1994), 9.
[2] Daniell, *Tyndale*, 23.
[3] Daniell, *Tyndale*, 22.

The scene into which he stepped was unique. About a decade earlier, a scholar named John Colet had returned from studies in Italy and had delivered a series of lectures at Oxford from 1496-1499 on the book of Romans.[4] His lectures were in Latin, the norm in a university setting, but his approach was anything but normal. Having been educated in Italy, he went through the text grammatically, in the way of the Italian humanists—certainly not the norm at Oxford.[5]

Colet's concept of justification was that of the Catholic Church—namely, that a man is justified on the basis of faith plus works—not by faith alone—so he cannot be considered a Christian, let alone a reformer. But his lectures conveyed the very important point that one did not have to become an expert in the classics in order to understand Scripture[6], and it seems to have sparked some sort of movement at Oxford in applying the Scriptures to the Christian life.[7]

Hard evidence on his whereabouts in the years immediately following Oxford, from 1516-1522, is also scarce. However, there is evidence that he spent some time at Cambridge University during this period, including a written

---

[4] Daniell, *Tyndale*, 32.

[5] Daniell, *Tyndale*, 35.

[6] At Oxford, no one was permitted study theology until they had completed the entire arts program up to the Masters' level, a structure was still in place a decade later when Tyndale arrived on the scene. Looking back on the experience in 1530, he wrote *"In the universities they have ordained that no man shall look in the Scripture until he be noselled in heathen learning eight or nine years and armed with false principles with which he is clean shut out of the understanding of Scripture."* Daniell, *Tyndale*, 37.

[7] Daniell, *Tyndale*, 36.

record from the pen of John Foxe, who places him at Cambridge between 1517 and 1521.[8]

While Cambridge was only separated from Oxford by a distance of 80 miles, the atmosphere could not have been more different, and it would have been a been a much better fit for Tyndale. Remember, 1517 was the year that Martin Luther had nailed his 95 theses to the door of the Castle Church in Wittenberg, Germany, and within only a few short years, Cambridge had become a hotbed for reformation theology. In fact, Tyndale's biographer David Daniell writes that Luther was so widely and so openly read among the Cambridge scholars that copies of his books were being publically burned as early as 1520.[9]

Tyndale may have attended Cambridge to improve his Greek. In 1516, the year before he may have arrived, Erasmus had published his Greek New Testament, and Cambridge was adding top-level Greek scholars to their faculty on an annual basis. He also may also have attended Cambridge to study divinity. Details are murky, but at some point between 1516 and 1522, Tyndale was ordained a priest,[10] and John Foxe wrote that at Cambridge, Tyndale *"further ripened in the study of God's Word."*[11]

In 1522, at the age of 28, Tyndale moved back to his childhood home of Gloucestershire and into Sodbury Manor, the home of Sir John Walsh, where he took a tutoring position for the Walsh children. The children were quite young, allowing Tyndale plenty of spare time, which he used to study

---

[8] *The Acts and Monuments of John Foxe*, 4th edn., ed. Revd Josiah Pratt, introd. Revd John Stoughton, 8 vols. (1877), v. 115.

[9] Daniell, *Tyndale,* 49.

[10] Daniell, *Tyndale*, 56.

[11] Daniell, *Tyndale*, 51.

Erasmus' Greek New Testament and to open air preach at St. Austin's Green, the town square.¹²

John Walsh was an influential and hospitable man who would often invite local clergy to his home for meals and conversation. Tyndale frequently joined them, but was often shocked by their lack of Biblical understanding, and became a source of irritation to many of the clergy because of his own knowledge of the Scriptures and his habit of asking pointed questions. In all likelihood he also became a source of anxiety for his hosts as he began to speak more freely of his plan to translate the Bible into the English language, something that was illegal at the time without permission from a high office in the church. Just over a century earlier, in 1408, the Constitutions of Oxford had outlawed the ownership of a vernacular Bible apart from the permission of the Bishop,¹³ and ownership of an English Bible remained illegal under that decree for 130 years, a period which encompassed the entirety of William Tyndale's life.

One well-known interaction between Tyndale and a visiting clergyman was recorded by Richard Webb:

> Master Tyndall happened to be in the company of a learned man, and in communing and disputing with him drove him to that issue, that the learned man said: "We were better be without God's law than the Pope's." Master Tyndall, hearing that, answered him: "I defy the Pope and all his laws;" and said: "If God spare my life, ere many years I will

---

¹² Daniell, *Tyndale*, 56.

¹³ http://www.bible-researcher.com/arundel.html (accessed on October 27, 2017).

cause a boy that driveth the plough shall know more of the Scripture than thou dost."[14]

It seems that the Scriptural ignorance of the clergy only fueled Tyndale's commitment to translate the Bible into English. In his introduction to his translation to the Pentateuch, he wrote,

> Which thing only moved me to translate the New Testament. Because I had perceived by experience, how that it was impossible to establish the lay-people in any truth, except the scripture were plainly laid before their eyes in their mother-tongue, that they might see the process, order, and meaning of the text: for else, whatsoever truth is taught them, these enemies of all truth (referring to the unqualified clergy) quench it again, partly with the smoke of their bottomless pit... and partly in juggling with the text, expounding it in such a sense as is impossible to gather of the text.[15]

Put simply: not only were the laypeople prevented by the Roman church from having the Scriptures in their own language, but to add insult to injury, those who were charged with teaching them the Scriptures were completely unqualified and incapable of the task. For Tyndale, there was only one solution: the people needed an English Bible.

---

[14] Daniell, *Tyndale*, 79.
[15] David Daniell, ed., *Tyndale's Old Testament* (New Haven: Yale University Press, 1992), 4.

In 1523, with the goal of printing an English Bible in view, Tyndale moved to London. The reason was simple: the Constitutions of Oxford outlawed the private ownership of a vernacular Bible without the Bishop's permission, and the Bishop lived in London. However, the timing was not on Tyndale's side. A special meeting of Parliament had recently been called by Lord Chancellor Cardinal Wolsey, who had recently engaged in an expensive war with France and now wanted bankrolling for another conflict. Parliament had granted Wolsey half the funds he had asked for, but had elected to raise the money through taxation, and London was full of resentment toward Wolsey; Tyndale biographer J.F. Mozley described Wolsey as "the best-hated man in the kingdom."[16]

As Bishop of London, Cuthbert Turnstall was fulfilling dual roles in church and state and had to handle the matter delicately, so when Tyndale sought his permission to live at his palace while translating the Scriptures into the English language, the risk was too much for Turnstall to bear. After all, this was 1523 – only two years after Martin Luther had been excommunicated by Pope Leo X and had refused to recant of his teachings at the Diet of Worms, and word of Tyndale's provocative conversations at Sodbury Manor in Gloucestershire may also have preceded him. Involvement in anything that could connect him with the schism forming in the Catholic Church would have been the last thing Turnstall needed or wanted,[17] and Tyndale's request was rejected.

---

[16] J.F. Mozley. *William Tyndale* (New York. The Macmillan Company, 1937) 37–38.

[17] Daniell, *Tyndale*, 86.

Tyndale was disappointed, but looking back we can see the providence of God at work. Tyndale didn't leave London immediately, instead taking a preaching position at St. Dunstan's in London while he contemplated his next move. There he met Henry Monmouth, who was also a native of Gloucestershire, but much more significantly, a member of the Merchant Adventurer's Company who engaged in wool-trading with Europe. Monmouth invited Tyndale into his home, the beginning of a providential relationship which would eventually see Monmouth using his connections within the shipping industry to help Tyndale smuggle his English Bibles into the country.

Tyndale came to realize that printing his English Bibles on the island was unlikely, and a move to mainland Europe would be necessary. He later wrote, *"I understood at the last not only that there was no room in my Lord of London's palace to translate the new Testament, but also that there was no place to do it in all England, as experience doth now openly declare."*[18]

Tyndale thus left the island to work on the mainland of Europe, arriving first in Hamburg, Germany. Hamburg, together with Antwerp and Cologne, was one of three great trading ports in Northeast Europe.[19] If Tyndale was going to translate, copy, and print the Bible and then smuggle copies back into England, he would need to know the ports well. And in fact, with the exception of two or three years in Worms and his imprisonment in Belgium at the end of his life, Tyndale would spend the rest of his days traveling between these three cities.

---

[18] Daniell, *Tyndale's Old Testament*, 5.
[19] Daniell, *Tyndale*, 108.

Tyndale was well-suited for the work of translation. He was an exceptional linguist, having command of no less than eight languages - Latin, Greek, German, French, Hebrew, Spanish, Italian, and English – and in God's providence, his upbringing had given him the sensitivity to the cultural and stylistic nuances that are so critical to the production of a translation that flows, that doesn't feel wooden. Across the nearby Severn River from his native Gloucestershire was the Gaelic region, and as a child, Tyndale would have been surrounded by dialects and cultural differences that had surely been used by the Lord to shape Tyndale into the linguist he would become.

In 1525, he moved to Cologne. There, he completed his English translation of the New Testament, and printing began at Peter Quentel's print shop. However, because of the loose lips of a couple of the printers at a local pub, the shop was raided. Tyndale and his assistant William Roye escaped and fled up Rhine River to Worms, but everything that had been printed was seized and destroyed.[20]

Printing resumed that same year, this time at a printing house Worms, and here, in the same city where Martin Luther had stood his ground only four years earlier at the Diet of Worms, Tyndale's first complete English New Testament in English was printed. Because of his connections with the cloth-making industry and the cooperation of Henry Monmouth and the Merchant Adventurer's Company, beginning in February 1526,[21] Tyndale was able to smuggle his New Testaments into England between layers of cloth on

---

[20] David Daniell, ed., *Tyndale's New Testament* (New Haven: Yale University Press, 1989), xi.

[21] Daniell, *Tyndale's New Testament*, 9.

textile shipments. The shipping channel took the boats down the Rhine River, across the English Channel, and up the Thames River to the port in London, where they were quietly received and distributed.

In London, Bishop Turnstall caught wind of what was happening. He banned the shipments, but not before about 3,000 copies had been printed. In an interplay that was almost comical, Turnstall would send spies to the docks to locate the shipments, use the Catholic church's money to purchase as many copies as possible to keep them out of the public's hands, and Tyndale would then use the church's money to finance further translation, revision, and printing.[22] In 1526, after intercepting an exceptionally large shipment, Turnstall celebrated with a special service at St. Paul's Cross in London, where he preached a sermon on why it is not necessary to have an English Bible before proceeding to burn the entire lot.

Between 1526-28 there is no clear evidence as to where Tyndale lived, but we know he was busy.[23] In 1527 he started writing books and tracts. In 1528 he published *The Parable of the Wicked Mammon,* an extended exposition on the parable of the unjust steward in Luke 16, which Tyndale used as a launching pad to write a doctrinal treatise on faith and works, stating that contrary to what the Roman church taught, salvation is by grace alone through faith alone in Christ alone.[24] Rome's response was "violent,"[25] and many were tortured and burned.[26] He also published "Obedience of a Christian Man," which was a response to Thomas More's

---

[22] Daniell, *Tyndale's New Testament,* 9; Daniell, *Tyndale,* 196-197.
[23] Daniell, *Tyndale,* 155.
[24] Daniell, *Tyndale,* 163.
[25] Daniell, *Tyndale,* 170.
[26] Daniell, *Tyndale,* 172.

charge that the reformers were teaching rebellion.[27] On the contrary, Tyndale showed, the Scripture require subjects to obey their masters. But Tyndale's greater point, yet again, was that in order for the subjects to know what the Scriptures required of them concerning their masters, they would need a Bible. By this time, Tyndale had also began his studies in the Hebrew language, with the goal of translating the Old Testament into English directly from the original text. In 1530, his translation of the Pentateuch came to print.

Details on his whereabouts between the Antwerp printings of "*Obedience of a Christian Man*" in 1528 and the Pentateuch in 1530 are scarce, but Foxe recounts a shipwreck Tyndale experienced on the way to Hamburg to print his translation of Deuteronomy which helps us put the pieces together.

> At what time Tyndale had translated the fifth book of Moses called Deuteronomy, minding to print the same at Hamburg, he sailed thereward (from Antwerp): where by the way, upon the coast of Halland, he suffered shipwreck, by the which he lost all his books, writings and copies, and so was compelled to begin all again new, to his hindrance and doubling of his labours. Thus having lost by that ship both money, his copies and time, he came in another ship to Hamburg, where at his appointment Master Coverdale tarried for him, and helped him in translating the whole five books of Moses, from Easter till December, in the house of a worshipful widow, Mistress Margaret van Emmerson, a great

---

[27] Daniell, *Tyndale*, 223–224.

sweating sickness being the same time in the town. So having dispatched his business at Hamburg, he returned afterward to Antwerp again.[28]

From Antwerp, Tyndale penned a number of booklets. In 1530, he wrote *The Pathway to the Holy Scripture*, a guide to reading Scripture.[29] In 1531 he published *An Answer Unto Sir Thomas More*.[30] Lord Chancellor Sir Thomas More was as opposed to the reformation as one could possibly be. He had helped King Henry VIII write his response to Martin Luther's challenge to the Roman church's sacramental system, and in three separate publications he had written nearly three-quarters of a million words against Tyndale. Tyndale, for his part, responded once, when he published his *Answer to More*, which ran a mere 8,000 words. Tyndale would not allow himself to be distracted from the work God had called him to do!

He followed up *Pathway to the Holy Scriptures* with three short expository tracts: *An Exposition upon the First Epistle of John* and *An Exposition upon the V, VI, VII chapters of Matthew* in 1531, and *A Brief Declaration of the Sacraments in 1533*.[31] As mentioned, his publication of the Pentateuch had emerged in Antwerp in 1530, and copies were in England by the summer. In 1531 he translated Jonah and made a revision of his earlier work on Genesis. In 1534 he printed his revised New Testament, which in the words of David Daniell, was "the glory of his life's work."[32]

---

[28] Daniell, *Tyndale*, 198.
[29] Daniell, *Tyndale*, 220.
[30] Daniell, *Tyndale*, 36.
[31] Daniell, *Tyndale,* 220.
[32] Daniell, *Tyndale's New Testament*, vii.

In the spring of 1535, Tyndale was betrayed by a young English student, Henry Phillips. Phillips had feigned friendship, gained Tyndale's trust, and subsequently betrayed him by identifying him to the authorities.[33] Tyndale was arrested and taken to Vilvoorde Castle near Brussels, where he was charged with heresy and imprisoned.[34]

In 1536, after 16 months in prison, it was time for him to go to his reward. Because he was an ordained priest, He was afforded the luxury of strangulation before being burned at the stake.[35] His last utterance before his life was taken was a prayer, asking that the King would allow a Bible in English: "*Lord, open the king of England's eyes.*"[36]

With that background in view, let's consider three aspects of Tyndale's life:

1. His steadfastness in his unwavering commitment to translate the Scriptures
2. His theology, which I'm going to propose was the ground of his steadfastness, and
3. His legacy.

Tyndale's Steadfastness

In 1522, 14 years before he died, in the house of John Walsh, he had told the visiting clergyman, "*If God spare my life, ere many years I will cause a boy that driveth the plough shall know more of the Scripture than thou dost.*" That was his siren call, his unwavering focus. It was his life. His every decision seems to have been made according to one principle: will it advance the cause of translating the Bible into the English language?

---

[33] Daniell, *Tyndale's New Testament*, ix.
[34] Daniell, *Tyndale's New Testament*, ix.
[35] Daniell, *Tyndale's New Testament*, ix.
[36] Daniell, *Tyndale*, 383.

His attendance at Cambridge for Greek studies and his later studies in Hebrew show his commitment to the integrity of the text. Over and over again it would come out in his writings. In a letter to John Frith written in January 1583, he once wrote, "*I call God to record, against the day we shall appear before our Lord Jesus, to give a reckoning of our doings, that I never altered one syllable of God's Word against my conscience, nor would do this day, if all that is in earth, whether it be honor, pleasure, or riches, might be given me.*"[37]

His commitment to the work is also seen in his complete disinterest in engaging in a long back-and-forth with Thomas More, whose writings against Tyndale totaled more than 750,000 words over a period of years. Tyndale rarely even responded. He was simply too focused on his work of translation. Then there was his rejection of Henry VIII's offer in 1531 to return to England as a scholar. Tyndale had been on the mainland for at least six years and missed his homeland dearly, and King Henry had extended the invitation to return. There was only one condition: Tyndale must stop all translation work immediately. Although he missed his homeland terribly, Tyndale refused.

Even while imprisoned in Vilvoorde Castle awaiting death, his focus was unwavering. In a letter to an officer of the castle, he wrote the following: "*I suffer greatly from cold in the head, and am afflicted by a perpetual catarrh, which is much increased in this cell... my overcoat is worn out; my shirts are also worn out... and I ask to be allowed to have a lamp I the evening: it is indeed wearisome sitting alone in the dark. But most of all I beg and beseech your clemency to be urgent with the commissary, that*

---

[37] Charles Taylor, *Calmet's Dictionary Of The Holy Bible*, 10th ed. (Crocker and Brewster. New York: 1956), 179.

he will kindly permit me to have my Hebrew Bible, Hebrew Grammar, and Hebrew Dictionary, that I may pass the time in that study."[38] Cold and cramped, sick and weary, and in all likelihood well aware of his impending death, he "begged and beseeched" the commissary "most of all" for his Hebrew Bible, Hebrew Grammar, and Hebrew Dictionary, in order to pass the time in study. *For Tyndale, every moment was redeemable.* Even Tyndale's final prayer, while tied to the stake in Vilvoorde awaiting strangulation, was simply one final cry for the advancement of the great cause to which he had given his life and was about to give his life: "Lord, open the king of England's eyes."

He was steadfast through persecutions: the treats, the raids, the betrayal by Henry Phillips, and the withering attacks from the pen of Thomas More. He was steadfast through hardships and discouragements, including (among many others) his rejection by Bishop Turnstall in London, the loss of his printed manuscripts when Peter Quentel's print shop was raided in Cologn, and his shipwreck on the way to Hamburg. What a stark contrast to the modern tendency of throwing up our hands and confidently declaring that it "must not be God's will" after the first sign of hardship!

He was not only steadfast through through persecutions and hardships, but also through many sorrows. Tyndale knew what was happening in England. Opposition was reaching fever pitch, and people were being burned alive after being converted through his writings. Tyndale's good friend John Frith was burned alive by Thomas More in 1531. That same year, Richard Bayfield, the man who ran the ships carrying Tyndale's writings to England, was discovered, arrested, and

---

[38] Daniell, *Tyndale's New Testament*, ix.

as Thomas More wrote gleefully, "well and worthily burned." John Tewkesbury, converted by reading Tyndale's "Parable of the Wicked Mammon" was whipped in More's garden, crippled on the rack, and burned. One James Bainham, when found to be in possession of all five of Tyndale's books, at first shrank back, denied the faith, and made a payment to Rome, but in 1532, under agony of conscience, went to Mass at St. Augustine's church in London and secured his place on Thomas More's burning stake by standing before the people with Tyndale's English New Testament in his hand, and as John Fox wrote, "declared openly, with weeping tears, that he had denied God."

These are but a sampling. David Daniell's biography contains name after name of simple believers whose lives were taken by Roman flames because they had been found in possession of Tyndale's writings. Tyndale knew what was happening. And yet, through these sorrows, he pressed on.

Tyndale's Theology
Secondly, there was his theology. Tyndale wrote:

> By grace, we are plucked out of Adam the ground of all evil and **graffed in(to) Christ, the root of all goodness**. In Christ God loved us, his elect and chosen, before the world began and reserved us unto the knowledge of his Son and of his holy gospel: and when the gospel is preached to us openeth our hearts and giveth us grace to believe, and putteth the spirit of Christ in us: and we know him as our **Father most merciful**, and consent to the law and love it inwardly

in our heart and desire to fulfill it and sorrow because we do not."[39]

Tyndale understood that it was through His Word that our "most merciful" God gives us His Spirit and "openeth our hearts and giveth us grace to believe." His theology is what drove his commitment to Scripture translation. Tyndale understood that the Word of God is not simply God's truth to a fallen humanity; it is the instrument by which the Spirit of God works in bringing His elect to saving faith.

Tyndale's Legacy
Finally there is Tyndale's legacy, which has come to us in the form of the 1611 King James Bible. In 1537, only months after Tyndale's martyrdom, in an astonishing turn, King Henry VIII licensed the first official English translation of the Bible, known as "Matthew's Bible." The name was an alias. It was a cover for Tyndale's friend John Rogers, who had put together Tyndale's published and unpublished manuscripts. Where Tyndale's Old Testament translation work was incomplete Rogers had supplemented with the work of Miles Coverdale, who had also published a translation in 1535.[40] In his short introduction to his translation of Tyndale's New Testament, David Daniell wrote "this, printed probably in Antwerp, is the real foundation of the English Bible. It reprints Tyndale's final revision of his 1534 New Testament, his 1530 Pentateuch, and the rest of his Old Testament work

---

[39] William Tyndale, *Selected Writings*, ed. David Daniell (New York: Routledge, 2003), 37.

[40] Tim Dowley et al, eds., *The History of Christianity. A Lion Handbook* (Hertfordshire: Lion Publishing, 1977), 397.

as far as Chronicles."[41] And two years later in 1539, the king's vice-regent Thomas Cranmer ordered the production of an ornate lectern Bible known as "the Great Bible" for use in all the churches. It was a slightly "Latinized" reworking of the Matthew's Bible, which was actually just Tyndale's translation with Coverdale filling in the blanks. Only three years after his martyrdom, Tyndale's work had been officially endorsed by the King.[42]

The political climate would soon change. In July 1553, Queen Mary I ascended the throne. A staunch Catholic and rabid opponent of the reformation, she ordered the burning of Christians en mass during her 5-yr reign. The first to be burned under Queen Mary was Tyndale's friend John Rogers, who had collected his manuscripts and overseen the publication of Matthew's Bible.

In 1560, the Geneva Bible appeared. Protestants escaping the reign of Mary had fled to Geneva at a time when Geneva (and Germany in general) was enjoying a massive renaissance of language study, and what was produced was a remarkable achievement. In addition to the text, the Geneva Bible had versification, editor's notes, illustrations, cross-references, maps, and a concordance. It was beautifully produced. The basis for the Geneva Bible was Tyndale.[43]

In 1604, King James called a 2-day conference at his palace to resolve a number of issues, and toward the end of the meeting, the Puritan side suggested the production of a new translation. It was now almost 50 years since the last great translation, and advances in language studies had been

---

[41] Daniell, *Tyndale's New Testament*, xi.
[42] Daniell, *Tyndale's New Testament*, xi.
[43] Daniell, *Tyndale's New Testament*, xii.

made. The purpose of the new translation was given right in its' preface: *"to make a good translation better."* The "good translation" was the Geneva Bible, the basis of which was Tyndale's work.[44]

In 1611 the Authorized Version was produced. David Daniel estimates that 83% of the 1611 King James Bible is pure Tyndale.[45] Daniel writes, "William Tyndale gave us our English Bible. The sages assembled by King James to prepare the Authorized Version of 1611, so often praised for unlikely corporate inspiration, took over Tyndale's work. Nine-tenths of the Authorized Version's New Testament is Tyndale's. The same is true of the first half of the Old Testament, which was as far as he was able to get before he was executed outside Brussels in 1536."[46]

Of the innumerable lessons we can glean from Tyndale's life, I will leave us with one: there are hills worth dying on. We all understand this, and we all takes stands on certain issues in life, and certain issues within the church. The problem is, we sometimes take stands on issues of secondary importance while surrendering or ignoring issues of primary importance. For Tyndale, the integrity of the Word of God and its centrality in the life of the church was a hill worth dying on. Today, the trend is often to downplay the centrality of God's Word in public and private life, and even in the life of the church, and elevate in its place the importance of subjective experience. Will we go the way of subjectivism as well, or will we take a stand with Tyndale, and more importantly with the inspired Biblical authors, who placed the

---

[44] Daniell, *Tyndale's New Testament*, xiii.

[45] Tyndale, *Selected Writings*, vii.

[46] Daniell, *Tyndale*, 1.

WILLIAM TYNDALE

Word of God at the very center of the life and practice of the church?

Scripture Index

Genesis
15:5–6 62
22 62

Exodus
33:19 94
34:6-8 94

Deuteronomy
4 37

Judges
7:2 68

Psalms
14:1 96
16:11 106
19:1, 3 95
100:3 87

Proverbs
30:5 34

Isaiah
29:13 106
48:9,11 100
66:2 118

Habakkuk
2:4 4

Matthew
3:13–17 47
4:17 112
5:28 70

6:11–12 114
7:3–5 119
10:37–39 116
15:19–20 70
19:26 117
23:23 117

Mark
1:14–15 112
1:4–15 112
10:17–22 115
10:18 84
12:17 9

Luke
6:43–45 83
16:17 33
18:9–14 69

John
1:14 98
3 88
3:16 55
8:28 98
14:9 36
15:19 9

Acts
2:1 2
2:42 2
4 5
4:11 3
5 5
7 5
7:1-53 3

Acts Continued
- 8 3
- 8:21 3
- 12 5
- 15 3
- 15:1 3
- 15:6 4
- 15:7–9 4
- 15:11 4
- 16 5
- 17:30, 34 112

Romans
- 1:20 96
- 1:23, 25 96
- 3:10–12 81
- 3:23 96
- 4:1–5 59
- 4:5 63
- 5:1–2 55
- 5:6–8 85
- 6:23 81
- 8:1–4 45
- 9:15–16 103
- 9:30–33 59
- 10:17 117
- 11:6 69
- 11:36 101

1 Corinthians
- 1:27–31 71
- 1:29 68
- 1:31 103
- 2:4–5 55
- 2:6–6 67
- 2:14 36
- 10:31 107

2 Corinthians
- 3:14 97
- 3:7-18 96
- 4 36
- 4:4 97
- 4:4–6 89
- 4:6 78
- 5:21 88

Galatians
- 2:20 113
- 5:1–5 56

Ephesians
- 1:3–14 102
- 1:4–6 88
- 2:1–10 79
- 2:8 .... 55, 103
- 2:8–9 .... 66, 67
- 2:10 87
- 2:2–3 82
- 4:11–16 120
- 4:13 120
- 4:18 81
- 5:25–28 85

Philippians
- 3:9 56

1 Thessalonians
- 2:13 33

2 Timothy
- 1:14 10
- 3:16 33
- 3:16–17 32

Titus
2:11.................................86

Hebrews
1:3...................................99
2:14–15, 17...................... 46
10:1–4............................. 44
10:5–10........................... 47
10:11–14......................... 48
10:19–23......................... 52

James
2:14–26....................... 59, 61
2:24............................ 54, 59

2 Peter
1:19..................................96
1:21..................................33

1 John
1:8–10........................... 114
2 9
4:10............................ 85, 88

Date Completed	Name

www.ingramcontent.com/pod-product-compliance
Lightning Source LLC
Chambersburg PA
CBHW061950070426
42450CB00007BA/1114